D0422016

The
Seven Principles
of Golf

Mastering the Mental Game
On and Off the Golf Course

DARRIN GEE

• • •

STEWART, TABORI & CHANG
NEW YORK

Published in 2007 by Stewart, Tabori & Chang
An imprint of Harry N. Abrams, Inc.

Text copyright © 2007 by Gee & Company, LLC
Illustrations copyright © 2007 by Keith Witmer

Excerpt from "Play by Pictures: Hit the Shots You Want by 'Seeing' Them
First," by Jack Nicklaus with Ken Bowden, from *Golf Magazine* (July 2000),
by permission of the publisher

All rights reserved. No portion of this book may be reproduced,
stored in a retrieval system, or transmitted in any form or by any means,
mechanical, electronic, photocopying, recording, or otherwise,
without written permission from the publisher.

Library of Congress Cataloging-in-Publication Data
Gee, Darrin.
    The seven principles of golf : mastering the mental game on and
off the course / Darrin Gee.
        p. cm.
    Includes bibliographical references and index.
    ISBN-13: 978-1-58479-582-7
    ISBN-10: 1-58479-582-4
    1. Golf. 2. Golf--Psychological aspects. I. Title.
GV965.G35 2007
796.352--dc22   2006028404

Editor: Jennifer Levesque
Designer: Pamela Geismar
Production Manager: Anet Sirna-Bruder

The text of this book was composed in Monotype Bell,
with Belizio and Trade Gothic.

Printed and bound in China

10 9 8 7 6 5 4 3 2 1

HNA

harry n. abrams, inc.
a subsidiary of La Martinière Groupe

115 West 18th Street
New York, NY 10011
www.hnabooks.com

*Dedicated with all my heart
to my wife, Darien,
who inspires me
to be true to myself and
aspire to reach my potential*

THE SEVEN PRINCIPLES OF GOLF

The First Principle: Get Grounded
Quiet the mind • Ground your body
Find your center

The Second Principle: Develop Feel
Slow down and notice • Make the connection
Do what feels right

The Third Principle: Visualize the Shot
Know what you want • Believe in what you want
See it happen

The Fourth Principle: Create Your Own Pre-shot Ritual
Create a personal ritual • Find your own space
Honor your ritual daily

The Fifth Principle: Find Your Natural Swing
Trust your instincts • Find your own way
Search your soul

The Sixth Principle: Play One Shot at a Time
Turn off the autopilot • Be present now
Surrender to the moment

**The Seventh Principle: Transform Your Golf Game,
Transform Your Life**
Trust the process • Embrace the journey
Transform your life

CONTENTS

INTRODUCTION

"Gowf is a place to practice fascination . . . our feelin's, fantasies, thoughts and muscles. All must join to play. In gowf ye see the essence of what the world itself demands . . . The game is a mighty teacher never deviatin' from its sacred rools, always ready to lead us on . . . And I say to ye all, good friends, that as ye grow in gowf, ye come to see the things ye learn in every other place . . . Ye'll come away from the links with a new hold on life, that is certain if ye play the game with all your heart."

Shivas Irons, *Golf in the Kingdom*
by Michael Murphy

IMAGINE hitting a solid drive down the middle of the fairway. With a perfect lie, you grab your favorite iron or fairway wood. Feeling confident that you'll not only hit the green, but get very close to the flag, you prepare for the shot. Just as you are about to swing, a thought enters your mind:

"Don't hit into the lake!"

Suddenly, you're tense, almost frozen. Feeling anxiety, pressure, or fear about hitting into the lake, you can't seem to clear these negative thoughts from your mind. Even though you're hitting your favorite club from a comfortable distance, with the same solid swing, the shot has suddenly become much more difficult.

Your mind has interfered. Filled with negative and defeatist thoughts such as "There's no way I'm going to clear that lake!" or "I always hit into the water," the mind has sabotaged your ability to perform.

As a golf coach, I've worked with thousands of golfers who "play" like seasoned professionals on the driving range. They hit beautiful shots almost on command, with picture-perfect finishes. However, when these same golfers step up to the first tee, things suddenly change. They begin to think about what they're doing, how they're doing it, and the consequences of not doing it right. Maybe they're remembering the last time they stood in that same place and reliving that experience in their mind. If a lake or sand trap happens to stand between them and the green, their attention—consciously or subconsciously—often shifts toward that lake or trap. You can guess where the ball is likely to end up.

Golf is a challenging mental exercise. One must be able to concentrate sporadically over a prolonged period of time, about four hours for an average round of golf. Sound like a long time? Well, consider this: how long do you think it takes to actually "play" golf, defined as actually swinging the club?

In our clinics, we hear everything from five minutes to an hour and a half. Try it for yourself or simply picture yourself playing a typical round of golf. Now count, from start to finish, how long it takes you to make a single swing. You'll probably come up with the same numbers as us: approximately *one to two seconds per swing*. Let's use an average of ninety shots, including putts, multiplying that by two seconds. Which means that during an average round of golf, you actually "play" golf (or swing the club) for about 180 seconds, or three minutes! So if you're only swinging a club for three minutes, then what are you doing for the other three hours and fifty-seven minutes?

Hopefully having fun, taking in the scenery and enjoying the company of your playing partners. However, more than likely, you are filling your mind with nonstop thinking, judging, overanalysis, and self-criticism of your swing and golf game. "What am I doing wrong?", "Is my head still?", "I need to keep my elbow in, my wrists cocked, my grip strong," "This is embarrassing!", or "Why can't I hit it like I did yesterday?"

Other distractions may also fill your mind. "This round is sooooo slow," "I better hurry up, people are waiting behind us," "My coach is watching," or "I just blew my entire score on that one hole!"

You may be distracted by non-golf-related thoughts. "I've got so much to do at work," "I wonder what we're going to eat for dinner," "I better not be late today, I should hurry up," or "I should be home with my kids."

When you finally reach your ball and it's your turn to hit, your mind is on overload. *Emptying your mind of all those thoughts is critical to hitting good shots.* With a crowded and busy mind, it will be difficult to focus and be present for the actual golf shot.

Concentrating for four hours straight is not only difficult, but virtually impossible. Even Tiger Woods says that he doesn't concentrate fully for four hours straight, but rather only when he needs to—right before and during each and every shot.

Simply put, a golfer only needs to concentrate for a few seconds at a time. The key is to be able to achieve this level of concentration on command *consistently* for each and every shot. This is how all players, at all levels, succeed in this game: *by playing one shot at a time.*

• • •

The mind is often filled with so many different thoughts that the body becomes totally confused. It doesn't know what you want it to do, and as a result, the body cannot complete the swing freely. Quieting the mind frees the body to do what it already knows how to do: make a smooth swing and hit the golf ball solidly. A quiet mind sets the stage for great golf shots.

All golfers, from seasoned professionals to beginning players, strive to improve their game. New gimmicks, contraptions, and swing methods are born every day, guaranteeing lower scores or your money back. Some may lead to short-term success or even marked improvement.

However, I believe there is one thing that can make perhaps the single greatest contribution toward improving your golf game (not to mention your experience of the game), and guess what? It's FREE. That's right. Often overlooked by the average player, professional golfers know it's the key ingredient to success, on and off the golf course. If you watch professional golf tournaments, you'll see that skill alone is not what separates the winner from the rest of the pack. It's the winner's ability to master the inner game, his or her mental and emotional states, even in moments of intense pressure. It's what fuels the comeback when a winner is trailing behind.

Everyone agrees that golf is 90 percent mental, and yet so few players actually devote any energy to improving this area of their game. During a PGA Teaching Professional convention, the audience was polled and asked, "How many people think golf is more mental than physical?" Everyone raised a hand. Then they were asked, "How many people practice their mental game more than their physical game?" No one raised a hand.

How much of your practice is dedicated to the mental game?

Mental game control is now considered one of the keys to achieving long-term improvement and satisfaction on the golf course. I prefer the term *inner game* as it implies more than just mental mastery; sometimes the best thing you can do for your game is to get out of your head and trust your body. The mind-body connection has long been researched and explored in various disciplines including martial arts, sports, dance, music, art, and medicine, and without a doubt it has its place in the game of golf.

Today, many touring professionals are practicing and applying an inner approach to their game, including sports psychology, relaxation techniques, and Eastern-based disciplines such as tai chi, chi gung, yoga, and meditation. A strong consensus is building, supporting the belief that a sound mental game is as important, if not more important, than a sound physical game. Tiger Woods learned mental strategy and techniques from his father early in life. Phil Mickelson rereads his college psychology notes on visualization to get an edge. Many players have personal yoga and meditation instructors, some of whom travel with the players while they are on tour.

In the past, professional golfers rarely spoke of sports psychology as a part of their regular practice and training. Today most speak of it routinely. Players are no longer embarrassed about having a sports psychologist or reading books on the inner game of golf. Many speak of it as the key to their success.

The shift toward inner-game preparation is happening now, not only on the professional level, but on all levels, especially for the everyday golfer. Why is this shift occurring and what is causing it? I believe every person's individual desire to achieve his or her potential, both on and off the golf course, is driving this shift.

Potential is the best that you can play. Remember those perfect shots you've hit, the ones that nail the sweet spot with effortless ease so that the ball just takes off, soaring into the air? Or think about your personal best round, when everything seemed easy and simple. These moments and personal best rounds are just whispers of your potential in the game of golf.

•••

So how do you discover your potential, and how do you play your best golf? This book will help you determine your own potential and begin the process of achieving it, both on and off the golf course.

I often ask my students, "What prevents you from playing your best golf?" Nearly everyone answers, "Inconsistency." One shot may be absolutely pure, while the next is a shank in the woods. One day they'll shoot their personal best; the next round is twenty strokes higher. Most golfers think consistency is hitting perfect shot after perfect shot.

Unfortunately, not even Tiger Woods, Jack Nicklaus, or Bobby Jones could manage that. However, what they could master was being consistent in their approach to every shot: *setting themselves up for the possibility* of hitting a perfect shot each and every time. A consistent approach, the right attitude, and a sound philosophy together provide a strong basis for hitting consistent shots and shooting lower scores.

Golfers vary in age, size, experience, and ability, but they share one thing in common: *passion*. Even when they're not playing golf, they're preoccupied with the game. Golfers often relive shots and rounds of golf in their minds. During meetings or sitting at the dinner table, golfers often have glazed looks on their faces, maybe thinking about that great wedge shot on 5, the birdie on 12, or the lip-out at 18 that kept them from breaking 80. They watch it more than they play it. When you turn on the TV in their homes, you'll find it on the Golf Channel.

Experiences on the golf course (i.e., feelings, emotions, actions) are deeply connected to how people live their lives off the golf course. How you carry yourself on the golf course reflects your true self. You've heard how golf is a perfect metaphor for life.

I find that my experiences on the golf course have had a direct parallel to my life off the golf course. After learning to play golf as a freshman in college, my game steadily improved over the years, with my handicap reaching the single digits. However, my game then hit a plateau, and then it got worse. My handicap ballooned, as did my frustration. I asked myself, "Why is this happening!?!"

I noticed that I was trying too hard. Attempting to be like better players, I tried to match their swings and styles. As a result, I fought my own swing, played poorly, and found little joy on the golf course. At the same time, in my professional career and personal life, I found myself trying to become someone I was not. While it seemed as if I had a lot of good things going for me on the outside, I was dissatisfied on the inside.

After taking a long break from the frustrations of golf, I later returned to the practice range and began to explore all parts of my game, including my inner game. During this process, I discovered my *natural swing*. I've been using it ever since, as I learned to enjoy the game once again. At the same time, I began to explore ways to improve my life off the golf course.

I ultimately created a career blending my passion for golf, my love for coaching, and my fascination for the inner game and how it can have a dramatic impact on every part of our lives, including golf. I now live happily on the Big Island of Hawaii with my wife and two children and share the Seven Principles of Golf with others every day at my Spirit of Golf Academy.

I believe that if you can take one ounce of your passion for golf or whatever you truly love and apply it to the rest of your experiences, you will surely lead a more fulfilling and gratifying life. Do you experience the same level of passion at home and work as on the golf course? Do you wake up in the morning, go to work, play with your kids, and love your partner with the same fervor? Simply becoming *more aware of how you play golf* will have a positive effect on all aspects of your life.

•••

The Seven Principles of Golf: Mastering the Mental Game On and Off the Golf Course will help you create a consistent, reliable way to quiet your mind and increase your focus and concentration for each and every shot, resulting in lower scores and more fun. By following one or all of the Seven Principles of Golf in our daily lives, we will begin to experience a more fulfilling and enriching life. As golfers, parents, spouses, and professionals, our outer personas or appearances are reflections of our inner selves. If we can be true to ourselves, then we can channel our pure energy and power toward creating fulfillment and prosperity in every part of our lives.

This book is divided into seven chapters, each one dedicated to one of the Seven Principles of Golf. Each chapter includes practical, easy-to-use exercises to help you put each Principle into regular practice. They will help you develop a strong mental game that will have an impact on every shot you take *for the rest of your life.* You may begin to experience golf at a whole new level, most likely resulting in better shots, lower scores, and more fun.

Each exercise is very simple and straightforward. They are designed to be explored at your own pace, one at a time or all together in sequence. You may find that one exercise will resonate with you more than others. If so, go with your instincts and use that Principle on the golf course. Many of the golfers I have coached apply the Seven Principles in a step-by-step process to every shot. Personally, depending on the situation, I apply different Principles as needed throughout the round of golf.

In each chapter, I also offer ways to apply these Principles to everyday living. You will see that these Principles are directly linked to other aspects of your life. Whether you're a professional golfer or a newcomer to the game, I hope you will gain great wisdom and knowledge from this book to apply to your life, or join us at our golf academy on the Big Island of Hawaii and experience the Spirit of Golf firsthand.

Darrin Gee
Kohala Coast, Island of Hawaii

GET GROUNDED

"You can will something to happen, with your body, with your mind. The mind is that strong. You can say, 'I want to get this close to the hole.' That's where the mind comes in. The mind has to produce positive thinking. All the great players do that."

Byron Nelson

GOLFERS take balance for granted. When my students set up for a golf shot, I frequently ask them if they feel balanced. After they have assured me that they are as balanced as they possibly can be, I give them a gentle, two-finger nudge and watch them topple over.

Most people think that if they are standing still, they are balanced. However, this theory quickly falls apart during the golf swing. If a golfer has not established a strong, well-balanced stance prior to swinging the golf club, he or she will have a difficult time striking the ball crisply in the sweet spot.

In most other sports, a balanced athletic stance is also required. Whether it be volleyball, tennis, basketball, football, or martial arts, you must be prepared to move in any and all directions, almost reflexively. Not knowing where your opponent or the ball will be going, you must have perfect balance at all times to respond accordingly. We can use that same thinking when playing golf.

I had one student who was an accomplished athlete in many sports, including basketball, football, and baseball. He was strong, quick, and had outstanding hand-eye coordination. He demonstrated outstanding balance in every sport he participated in, *except golf.* When he addressed the ball, he was off-center, often leaning back on his heels. When he swung the club, he often finished out of balance, wobbling around while trying to remain standing.

Golf is a "still" sport. You are primarily stationary, which means that balance in golf is even more important than in other sports. In most other sports, if you lose your balance, you can move your feet to regain it and resume play. In the game of golf, the swing takes less than two seconds. In such a short period of time, you don't have time to move your feet and adjust. Shifting your entire weight from one side of your body to the other, without moving your feet, while swinging a golf club and trying to hit a tiny ball, is probably one of the most difficult motions in sports to master.

I believe that balance, or getting grounded, is the core and foundation of the golf swing. A golfer may have a beautiful, fluid swing, but if it's coupled with poor balance, the result is often an off-center shot. You must first establish a grounded, balanced stance as the basis for a solid golf swing.

•••

You often see professional golfers shuffling their feet around, rocking back and forth, and adjusting their stance in preparation for a shot. This is often misunderstood as a nervous habit, but more often than not they are just trying to find their balance and establish solid grounding before making their swing.

A student of mine named Don visited me at our golf academy, desperately wanting help with his golf game. He and his buddies had all started playing golf at about the same time. His friends seemed to improve, while he did not. He often felt embarrassed by his poor play and worried what others thought about him and his game. Compounding the situation, he doubted his golf swing and often found himself having a million different swing thoughts before, during, and after a shot. As a result, he often tightened up during his swing, hitting more dirt than ball.

Don had taken lessons, read golf instruction books and magazines, and tried several swing aids and gimmicks. He improved a little each time, but always regressed back to his original ability,

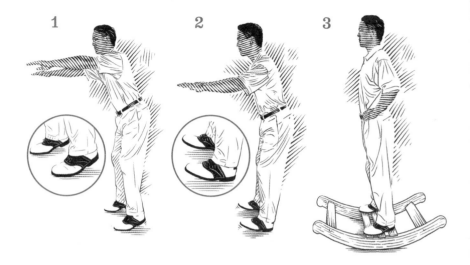

sometimes even getting worse. Because of his struggles with the game, he nearly quit, until I shared with him a few things about quieting the mind, finding his balance, and trusting his body.

Don had a lot on his mind, both golf- and non-golf-related thoughts. He often rushed his shot in an attempt to "get it over with." He rarely took the time to establish a sound foundation. As a result, he often lost his balance during his swing and rarely made solid contact with the ball.

I asked him to get as balanced as possible as he set up to the golf ball. Once he said he felt balanced, I gave him a soft push on his shoulder. He nearly fell over. Don needed to improve his balance and learn how to ground his body.

First, I had him stand on his toes and lean forward, while maintaining his balance throughout his body. [1] Then I had him lift up his toes and stand on his heels. [2] This proved to be very challenging to him. I then asked him to rock back and forth, heel to toe, toe to heel, imagining that he was a rocking chair. [3] This exercise helped him gain a better sense of balance and rhythm. I told

him to slow down and shorten the rock- 4
ing motion until he reached an equilibrium
point between his toes and heels.

He then repeated the same exercise
laterally, or sideways. Finally, I had him
make small circles with his hips. As he was
doing this, I told him to imagine circling
around the center of his body. I told him to
make smaller and smaller circles, spiraling
until he reached the center point.

At this point, he had essentially found
his center. However, this was not enough.
In order to lock in this feeling of total balance, I told Don to imagine the spikes in
his golf shoes growing into the ground like the roots of a tree. [4]
Using the imagery of roots growing down and spreading in all
directions helped him establish a solid foundation. I had him put
particular emphasis on the balls of his feet, which gave him a solid,
grounded feeling.

I asked him to swing his arms back and forth around his body,
while keeping his feet firmly planted. He built a strong foundation,
and yet he was completely loose and flexible on top. Using the imagery of a palm tree or willow tree, Don was able to achieve a balance of
strength and flexibility, exactly what is needed for the golf swing.

With his eyes closed, Don learned to maintain his balance and
notice the difference between "thinking" he was balanced and actually "being" balanced. By focusing on his feet and legs being firmly
rooted into the ground, he improved his swing dramatically. And
yet his swing was essentially the same: what changed was his balance. What was once a swaying, imbalanced, and off-centered swing
became a solid, flowing, and effortless motion.

I told him to close his eyes and practice his swing. He could immediately discern the difference between good and poor balance. When he concentrated on his feet and legs being rooted into the ground, he had better balance. If he thought of anything else, he lost his balance.

When Don started hitting golf balls after this exercise, he hit them with both precision and accuracy. His shots lofted in the air like he had never seen before. He was amazed. The First Principle of Golf, Get Grounded, helped Don focus on establishing a strong connection between his body and the ground, which led to solid swings.

•••

How is *your* balance? There are a few simple ways to test its quality. Standing on one foot with your eyes closed is an exercise that will give you feedback on your balance. Notice how you must adjust to find the perfect balancing point. You may wobble a bit, but this exercise will help you establish better balance for future golf swings. Remember to do this with each foot, as we often favor our stronger leg first. You want to feel so grounded that you would be able to maintain your balance on uneven lies and in gusty and windy conditions.

Making practice swings with your eyes closed will also help you find your balance. Notice how your feet and legs must work diligently to maintain your balance throughout the swing. This is no different when your eyes are open. Keep swinging with your eyes closed, until it feels smooth, rhythmic, and flowing. Then take a few swings with your eyes open and notice how your balance has improved.

Another way to achieve better balance is through an exercise called the two-foot jump stop. Used in almost all sports, including basketball, baseball, tennis, and volleyball, this exercise teaches you how to achieve a solid, balanced stance without trying or thinking.

5

[5] Take a few steps in succession followed by a short hop, landing with both feet on the ground simultaneously. Allow your knees to bend and flex naturally. You may find that when you land, you have the majority of your weight on the balls of your feet or slightly forward. Let your arms dangle. This is a very natural stance and perfect for the golf swing.

If you lean too far forward during this exercise, you'll fall over; if you lean too far backward, you'll get jolted back. With a few repetitions, this exercise will help you find perfect balance.

EXERCISES

1. Finding a comfortable stance, stand tall on your toes. Gently lean forward as far as you can while maintaining your balance, and hold for ten seconds.

2. Reverse your weight to your heels and raise your toes up, using your arms as necessary to maintain your balance, and hold for ten seconds.

3. Rock back and forth from heel to toe, toe to heel. Imagine you are a rocking chair as you are rocking back and forth. Just like a rocking chair, your rocking motion will shorten and slow down, eventually stopping at the equilibrium point, where there is equal weight distributed between the toe and heel.

4. Rotate your hips round and round, making small circles. Switch directions, and with each successive circle getting smaller and smaller, you are going to spiral until you reach the center. Settle and sink into this position.

5. Imagine the spikes in your golf shoes growing deep into the ground, as if you are a tree with roots spreading underground. Put particular emphasis and awareness on the balls of your feet, imagining those two roots anchoring and connecting deeply to the core of the earth. Feel the energy and power in your feet, calves, thighs, hips, and lower abdomen. Notice how strong a foundation you have created.

》》》

6. Swing your arms freely around your body, while maintaining this strong foundation. Imagine a palm tree, willow tree, or bamboo reed, with a solid and strong foundation, yet extremely flexible on top, able to bend and twist easily. This is exactly what you want for the golf swing.

GET GROUNDED
OFF THE GOLF COURSE

Quiet the mind
Ground your body
Find your center

The First Principle of Golf: Get Grounded also has significant implications for your life off the golf course. For example: Have you ever experienced a sense of being overwhelmed by life and your responsibilities? Are you constantly trying to balance your career with family and feel like you're not quite succeeding? Do you never seem to have any time just for you? If you answered yes to any or all of these questions, then you are definitely a member of the human race and probably in need of a little more balance in your life.

We are always attempting to organize and prioritize the many parts of our lives, often with temporary or limited results. Job, family, relationships, money, lack of free time—it never seems to cease. And even if we do manage to get ahead, it's short-lived. New things demand our attention. Surprises and unexpected events occur. We end up back where we started, barely keeping up, doing what we can just to keep it together so that we have some semblance of an acceptable, normal life.

Greg has been one of my regular clients for the last several years. When he first attended the Spirit of Golf Academy, he was experiencing many challenges in his life. He was exhausted from working seventy-hour weeks, his health was deteriorating, and he was financially overextended, with a huge mortgage and two children in college. In addition to that, his golf game was at an all-time low.

The stresses in Greg's life carried over to his golf game. Like every player, from beginners to tour professionals, he experienced tense situations on the golf course. The first tee jitters, hurrying to keep pace with the fast group behind, or being angry at how poorly he was playing were common. He rarely enjoyed the game and experienced frustration time and again.

At delicate times like these, he could figuratively topple over the edge with just a slight nudge. Any combination of negative events could lead to an emotional outburst. Greg needed some tools that could help him return to a more balanced and centered state of mind. One of the best tools to use in any stressful situation, on or off the golf course, is to slow down . . . everything. Slow down your breathing, slow down your walking, and slow down your mind.

In life, the mind fills with so many thoughts of what to do that you tend to float from one task to another with very little awareness. The best way to establish balance in your life is to quiet your mind and establish a strong feeling of connection.

In Eastern philosophy, balance and the flow of energy (chi) are imperative to good health, vitality, and well-being. They are the basis of many martial arts practices. In Chinese medicine, doctors look for whatever may be "out of balance" and then suggest remedies that will bring your body back "into balance." They don't need fancy machines or elaborate tests to pinpoint the problem: all the information they need is contained within the body.

Our tendency is to look outside of ourselves for the solution (golfers are especially guilty of this). What can we buy? What is everybody else doing? What worked for Bob? What worked for Beth? How much does it cost and how long will it take?

You've probably figured out what I'm going to say next, which is that the best tool available is within you. *Quiet your mind and trust your instinct and intuition.* Greg began to slow down in his life. He took up tai chi and practiced meditation regularly. He felt more at ease and relaxed, while at the same time he became more energetic and alert. He learned to seek balance in all parts of his life. Once balance was restored in his mind, he began to make better decisions and choices. As a result, his life improved . . . and so did his golf game.

In a magazine interview, Tiger Woods said, "To me, it's all about balance . . . If I feel something is out of balance, I try to get it back in balance somehow. Your entire life, you're always working to keep everything in balance, because the more harmony there is, the smoother life goes."

•••

1. *QUIET THE MIND.* The Chinese have a saying that translates into "monkey mind," the constant chatter that seems to fill every crevice of your mind. The monkey mind is always at work and always has something to say. The monkey mind doesn't need much of a break, which means *you* don't get much of a break, either. One of the best ways to overcome monkey mind is to *practice quiet moments.* Try sitting quietly with your eyes closed, meditating, going for a walk, or exercising without reading or watching TV. Practice tai chi or yoga. Turn off the music, talk radio, and cell phone when you are in the car commuting to work. These are all effective ways to develop an experience of calm and relaxation. With practice, your mind and body will begin to crave those quiet moments and know how to achieve them when necessary.

»»

2. GROUND YOUR BODY. Notice how your body physically connects you to the ground. Wherever you are, whether at home, in the car, on an airplane, in the golf cart, or in the office, plant your feet firmly to the ground. Notice the weight and mass of your body molding into your seat. Place your feet solidly onto the floor and imagine them rooting into the ground. This practice will give you a sense of being grounded and building a solid foundation. You can practice this anywhere, at any time, even if you're just standing in line at the market.

3. FIND YOUR CENTER. As you ground yourself, notice where your energy is centered. Is it in your head, in your chest, or in your legs? Begin to focus your energy toward the spot two inches below your navel, in between the front and back of your body. This is called the *hara* in Japanese, or *dantien* in Chinese. In martial arts, this is considered the center of your body. With each breath continue to focus on the *hara*, inhaling and exhaling from your center. Feel the energy or chi emanating from this center, creating a strong connection with your body.

DEVELOP FEEL

"Golf is a difficult game, but it's a little easier if you trust your instincts. It's too hard a game to try to play like someone else."

Nancy Lopez

FEEL is one of the most important factors in developing a solid, all-around golf game. You often hear television golf commentators describe tour professional golfers as having great "touch" or "feel" in their short game and putting. What they are talking about is how tour professionals have the ability to tune into their senses and vary their level of exertion, even though they are making the same basic motion.

For example, if a tour professional is in the rough near the green, he or she will often take a full-speed swing with a lob or sand wedge, hitting the ball gently into the air and landing it softly on the green. The professionals do this by establishing a connection with the club and a feel for the shot.

In the game of golf, each individual club performs a certain function. The driver is used to hit the ball long distances off the tee. The long irons are for hitting the ball off the fairway in a low-boring trajectory. The short irons are for precise, high-trajectory shots determined to land and stop on the green. Each club is intended to launch the ball a certain distance with a particular trajectory.

However, there is one club in your bag that does not have a specific distance associated with it—the putter. Because the putter must produce shots of an infinite number of distances, it is a great tool with which to begin developing feel.

Many of my students confess that putting is their greatest

weakness. They have difficulty in determining how hard or soft to hit the ball. One student named Sidney said she could never figure out distance, often hitting the ball far beyond the cup. Worse yet, she constantly received advice from friends and relatives, all of whom claimed to have the answer to her putting woes, which confused her even more.

Sidney needed simple advice. I suggested that she focus on the "feel" in her hands. She wasn't sure what I meant. I asked her to hold her putter and evaluate her grip on a scale of 1 to 10, with 1 being a "feather-light" grip and 10 being a "white-knuckle death" grip. She said she held the club at an 8.

As it turned out, Sidney gripped all her clubs on the tighter side. You may notice that if you grip a club tightly, your flexibility decreases. The tighter your grip, the less flexible you are and vice versa. And with a tighter grip, not only do your hands tighten up, but so do your forearms, shoulders, neck, and back. In fact, your entire body tenses up to some degree when you have a tight grip.

Grip pressure is unique to each individual. Experiment with varying degrees of tightness or looseness in your grip, and notice how the flow of your swing changes. Find out which grip pressure allows you to swing in the most relaxed and free-flowing motion.

Sam Snead, one of golf's legends, imagined holding a live bird while gripping the club. He imagined this not only at the beginning of the swing, but from start to backswing to follow-through. [SEE 6, NEXT PAGE] In his mind, if he held the bird too tight, he would hurt it, and if he held it too loose, it would fly away. This translates into a grip pressure of 2 or 3.

Sidney discovered that with a lighter grip, she relaxed more, allowing her arms to hang loosely from her body. I also emphasized that when she relaxed her hands, a domino effect took place—not only were her hands more relaxed, but so were her arms, shoulders, back, hips, and legs. This would allow her to swing more freely.

6

Inversely, if she tensed up her hands, her arms, shoulders, and the rest of her body would also tighten up.

With a lighter grip, she began to allow her arms to move more naturally, back and forth in perfect rhythm like the arm of a grand-father clock. [7] She said she could now notice how the putter "felt"—the contours and texture of the putter grip, the weight of the putter head, how her hands were interconnected with each other. This was a clear sign that she had heightened her awareness and sensitivity, developing the ability to feel and connect with the club. She was much more comfortable and con-fident. As a result, she no longer thought about how hard to hit the ball. She just allowed her arms to flow freely, which translated into quality putts.

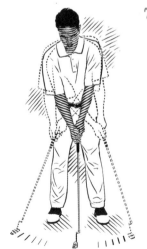

7

There are many ways to develop feel

or touch. On the putting green, find your optimal grip pressure by hitting ten consecutive putts from the same spot one foot away from the cup. Start with a 1 grip and work your way up to a 10. Determine which grip pressure feels the best and most comfortable. More than likely, it will be lighter than your regular grip pressure, leading to better touch or feel.

This also applies to the full swing. Often during our clinics, golfers have a difficult time keeping a relaxed grip throughout the swing. They may start with a 2 grip, but by the time the club hits the ball it's up to a 9 grip. Prior to making full swings, grip the club as tightly as possible and then relax your grip pressure. Swing with that lighter grip. You will notice that it is much easier to maintain a lighter grip throughout your swing.

Maintain the same grip pressure during the entire swing from start to finish. By doing so, you will stay relaxed throughout the swing. If you tighten your grip ever so slightly during your swing, your entire body will tighten, which will have a dramatic impact on the quality of your shot.

Another way to heighten your senses and develop feel is to listen. On the putting green, listen for the ball falling into the cup. By listening for the rattle of the ball in the cup, you begin to train your body to create that sound. It becomes a part of the process of putting and you will perform at a higher level.

Joan consistently lifted her head up to see where the ball was going, be it on the putting surface or on the fairway. As a result, she often topped the ball. She had tried every method to keep her head down, at times resorting to lowering her chin to touch her chest. Nothing worked, and the more people told her to keep her head down, the more she lifted up. Instead of "trying" to keep her head down, I asked her to simply listen . . . listen for the sound of the golf ball rattling into the bottom of the cup. For full swings and chips, I told her to listen for the "click" of the club striking the ball. By listening, she naturally kept her head stable and no longer felt the need to look up.

By listening for the sound of the club striking the ball, you can also tell how well you hit the ball. Every golf club has a sweet spot, a specific place on the club that is designed to connect with the ball for optimal performance. The sweet spot on most modern-day putters is identified by a line or dot. When you connect the sweet spot of the club with the ball, you will often hit more solid shots. You will also notice that this connection creates a solid sound. With a higher level of awareness, you'll be able to determine the quality of your shot, just by listening.

You can also feel shots. After you strike a ball, whether on the green or the fairway, notice how it felt. Did it vibrate or shake in your hands? Or was it seemingly light, as if you hadn't even swung the club? This will provide you with immediate feedback on how well you hit the ball.

There are a few games you can play on the golf course that will help you become a more creative, feel-based golfer. I took one student, Jane, out for a playing lesson. She was extremely mechanical and calculated every angle for every shot. On her approach shot on the par-4 first, she asked me how far it was from her ball to the flagstick. I was silent. She asked again, and I responded by asking her not to look for yardage markers or guess the distance.

"Select a club based on feel," I said. "Choose the club that feels right." She looked at me as if I was crazy. "How am I supposed to pick a club when I don't even know how far I am? I know that if I am a certain distance, I will hit a certain club. Without that information, I can't be certain."

I looked at the hole and said, "Can you ever be 100 percent certain? With the same club, does every shot go exactly the same distance every time? Some days you may hit a particular club one distance, and other days it may be ten yards less or more. Choose your club by feel or intuition at this moment." She stared at the hole and looked at her irons. "Don't think. Just choose. And trust it totally." She chose her club with confidence and took dead aim. With a confident swing, she struck the ball solidly, landing it pin-high, six feet from the cup.

Play a few holes or even an entire round of golf choosing clubs based on what feels right. Ignore the yardage markers. Trust your intuition. Feel your way around the golf course. You may find that you'll fare just as well, if not better.

Expand your creativity. Technically, you can use any club at any time on the golf course. For example, from ninety yards, you can hit virtually any club in your bag. You can hit a high–flying wedge, a knocked-down 8-iron, or a 5-iron bump-and-run. You could even putt the ball, especially if you're playing a course where the fairways and greens are cut close. Use your feel and intuition, spark your creativity, and discover a whole new relationship to the game of golf.

EXERCISES

1. Hold your putter as if you were about to make a putt. Determine your grip pressure on a scale from 1 to 10, with 1 being feather-light and 10 being the death grip.

2. Now grip the club as tightly as possible. Take a practice putt and notice how it feels. Next, grip it as lightly as possible—so lightly that it almost slips out of your hand. Take another practice putt and notice how it feels.

3. Starting with a feather-light 1 grip, take a practice putting stroke. Then increase the grip pressure to 2 and take another stroke. Continue this exercise until you reach the grip pressure that is most comfortable. The key is to maintain that grip pressure throughout the entire motion from start to backswing to follow-through.

4. Imagine the club as an extension of your arms, extending all the way down to the putter head. Close your eyes, and set the club in motion. Allow your arms to move slowly, back and forth in a natural pendulum-like motion. Imagine the movement as that of the arm of a grandfather clock.

5. Let your arms flow naturally, back and forth. Notice how it feels, how effortless and easy it is, once you let the club do the work. Keep practicing until you feel as if you've made a perfect stroke. You will know when it happens.

6. Set up to a ball six inches from the hole. Clear your mind of all thoughts. You may feel an urge to think, "How hard do I need to hit the ball?" *Don't.* Just focus on the feel in your hands and the rhythmic movement of your arms.

7. Find your balance, relax your grip, and let it flow. Trust your body and let the club hit the ball. Allow your arms, hands, and the club to move instinctively.

8. Continue with this process, rotating around the hole and moving the ball out to one foot, one and a half feet, two feet, two and a half feet, etc., until you reach six feet. [8]

8

9. Notice if you make a solid connection between the club and the ball. Did it feel like you hit the sweet spot?

DEVELOP FEEL
OFF THE GOLF COURSE

Slow down and notice
Make the connection
Do what feels right

Feel or intuition is innate. However, in the Western world we are often taught to ignore our intuition in favor of the "facts." We have all made decisions based on logic and reason rather than on intuition, only to regret our choices later.

Everyone has experienced intuitive moments during his or her life. Young children are the best examples of intuitive behavior and pure authenticity in action. What they do comes naturally. They seek out what feels good and is interesting, and avoid the opposite. They take curiosity to experimentation, without fear or hesitation. They laugh and cry whenever they feel like it.

As children grow older, they begin to limit themselves to boundaries set by school and social pressure. "Good" behavior that falls within set boundaries is rewarded, while creativity and individualism are discouraged. They are told what to do, when to do it, and how to do it. If they deviate, act up, or speak out of turn, they are punished.

A librarian shared how she often hears parents tell their children which books to choose. "You don't want that book. You want this one." I am sure parents are doing this with their children's best interest in mind. However, they are sacrificing their children's intuition and creativity. As an adult, you may be continuing this childhood pattern, limiting yourself and suppressing your intuition.

You may be holding back, telling yourself that you don't need or deserve what you truly want.

Advertising influences people to buy products and services, as simple as cereal, automobiles, and personal computers, whether they truly want them or not. Today, quantitative research (i.e., surveys, polling, focus groups) has become a key tool in helping companies determine how to tweak products and services so that they end up in the marketplace and in our homes.

A top marketing executive at one of the largest food companies in the world once told me that while this type of data is critical in decision-making, oftentimes the best decisions are not based solely on quantitative analysis, but rather more importantly on conviction, gut feel, and instinct.

We regularly face challenging decisions such as which house to buy, which college to choose, or whether to have more children. Think about the last difficult decision you had to make. In these situations, we often spend far too much time gathering data, analyzing that data, and comparing the pros and cons of each option. Even for seemingly simple choices such as selecting the color of a new car or where to eat dinner, we tend to overanalyze, which clouds decision-making. When making decisions, consider the alternatives, review the information on hand, and then make your choice based on what feels best. More often than not, the intuitive decision is the right choice.

You have experienced intuitive, deep-rooted moments without knowing it. Perhaps it was when you first met your future spouse and knew he or she was "the one," or when you decided to invest in a seemingly risky business deal. When everyone else said, "No, don't do it," your instincts said, "Yes, it's a great deal." During experiences like these, if we quiet our minds and trust our instincts, we often know exactly what to do.

Trust your instincts and allow your inner voice to speak out loudly and clearly. Anytime you need guidance, listen attentively to your inner voice and most of your questions will be answered.

•••

1. SLOW DOWN AND NOTICE. The best place to start is with your thought process. When confronted with a stressful situation, difficult decision, or trying experience, take a few deep breaths and close your eyes. Sit in silence, even for just a few seconds. Slow down your thoughts, and the stress and difficult situation will begin to lighten, allowing you to respond with more clarity, focus, and purpose.

2. MAKE THE CONNECTION. One of the best ways to develop feel is to connect the conscious mind with the subconscious mind. Practicing meditation, martial arts, yoga, or aerobic exercise allows one to get into a flow. When the mind, body, and spirit are working together, one is able to achieve a higher level of awareness.

3. DO WHAT FEELS RIGHT. "Go with your gut instinct." This common saying goes beyond following a simple hunch. There is a physical connection between the body and your deeper intuition. Focus on how you respond to challenging situations. Look to your body for physical signals such as uncomfortable or awkward sensations, or feelings of authenticity and rightness. Use these cues as a guide for making choices in your life. Your body will guide you. Perhaps you are searching for an answer. Ask yourself the question, and without conscious thought or analysis, listen to your inner voice and the answer will slowly reveal itself to you.

VISUALIZE THE SHOT

"I close my eyes and see the shot. I look at the ball and see the type of shot I have in my mind. I see it fly and then I see it land. It's a way of seeing the result before you do it. I visualize the end result."

Annika Sorenstam

VISUALIZATION, a technique used by professional athletes, as well as artists, dancers, and performers, is a simple yet profoundly powerful tool that will help you create what you want. By envisioning what you truly desire, you prepare your body to perform at a higher level to create it. In the game of golf, players of all abilities can use visualization to create the shots they want.

Professional golfers always picture in their mind's eye the shot they want to create prior to executing the shot. The more detailed the visualization, the higher the probability that they will create that shot.

Many people have practiced visualization in their daily lives, without even realizing it. For example, at this moment, imagine what your home looks like. See the details of the front door, the windows, and the roof. Picture the color of the house and the front yard or entranceway. This is visualization—seeing it in your mind. You can also visualize objects in motion, like a plane taking off or a racing horse or a golf ball taking flight.

In the game of golf, visualization is critical. I've broken down visualization into three simple steps:

1. Knowing what you want

2. Picturing or visualizing what you want (the path of the ball) in your mind's eye

3. Trusting and committing to that visualization 100 percent

Step 1—Knowing what you want

Knowing what you want is often overlooked. During playing lessons on the golf course, if a student misses a putt and appears upset, I often ask him or her, "Before you hit the ball, what did you have in mind, what did you want to happen?" After contemplation, the majority of students answer, "I guess I just wanted to get it close to the hole." My response is, "Then you shouldn't be disappointed, because you got exactly what you wanted."

Be specific about what you want. When putting, you want the ball to go into the hole. Even if it is fifty feet away, there is a possibility that it could go in. Pinpoint your desired outcome even further. For putting, specify the particular spot of the cup where you want the ball to enter. For a shot on the fairway, pick the exact spot where you want your ball to finish. Not just anywhere on the fairway or green, but at a specific spot.

The key to visualization is to focus on what you want rather than on what you don't want. In other words, envision the type of shot and outcome you would like to create, rather than negative outcomes.

How many times have you said to yourself, "Don't hit it in the water, don't hit it in the water, don't hit it in the water," only to end up hitting it in the water? If you focus on what you *don't* want, you often manifest it! Instead, focus on what you want, such as the ball landing on the green at a specific spot, bouncing, and rolling to your desired location, perhaps even into the hole.

Considered to be one of the best golfers in modern times, Phil Mickelson has often experienced difficulty in creating the shots that he wanted at crucial moments. A few years ago, he felt the need to review some visualization techniques he learned earlier that might get him back on track. He dug up his old psychology notes from college and relearned an important lesson on visualization.

He discovered how his mind was interfering with his game. "In the past, my mind would wander and I would start seeing shots that I didn't want to hit. I was working out of a more negative frame of mind. By simply visualizing what I want to occur, I have been able to pull off those shots," Mickelson said.

Phil realized that he had been visualizing poor outcomes, rather than the shots he wanted. The confusion in his mind affected the quality of his golf shots. Once he switched to visualizing the positive shots he wanted, his game and approach to golf changed dramatically.

Step 2—Picturing or visualizing the path of the ball in your mind's eye

After determining what you want, picture in your mind's eye the exact path of the ball from start to finish. In putting, simply picture how the ball will travel from point A (the ball's current location) to point B (the bottom of the cup). Will it go absolutely straight or will it curve in a particular direction? Will it travel slowly and deliberately or will it charge into the back of the hole?

With the exercises at the end of this chapter, you may discover that you have an innate ability to read breaks and judge the speed of greens with minimal thought or calculation. A student named Mike took about two minutes before every putt, looking at it from every angle, judging the wind, grain, slope, and who knows what else. It was if he was calculating a complicated equation or spreadsheet model that would tell him exactly how to hit the ball.

One time after he had gone through his laborious calculation, I asked him to erase that image and start over again. This time I told him to take a quick, two-second glance at the ball and the hole and not to think too much. What did he see? He said he saw essentially the same exact line. His intuition proved to be just as powerful as his scientific calculation.

On the Golf Channel's series *Playing Lessons from the Pros*, PGA Touring Professional Jeff Sluman, one of the top players in the game, talked about the power of intuition on the greens. He confessed that during pro-ams held on Tuesday or Wednesday before a tournament, he rarely took much time to read a putt. He basically gave it a quick look, set up to the ball, and let it go. More often than not, the results were outstanding. On the other hand, during actual tournaments, he tended to read putts from all sorts of angles, calculate all the variables, and consult with his caddie, only to find that his putting fared no better and perhaps even worse than during the pro-ams. He believes that often people just overthink these things.

Here are a few suggestions to develop or improve your visualization skills. Try standing behind the ball, with the hole on the opposite side. As you gaze at the area surrounding the ball and hole, look at the big picture, keeping a soft focus in your eyes. Do not look at anything in particular, such as a blade of grass or a dimple on the ball; just maintain a soft, almost blurry view. Slowly, the path or line may begin to appear in your mind's eye. [9]

9

Personally, I see a half-inch-thick, fuzzy white line that leads from the ball into the hole. My intuition tells me exactly the path of the ball. If it is straight, I visualize a straight line; if there is some break, I visualize a curving line.

Everyone "sees" something different when it comes to visualization. One student at our golf school visualized a string joining the ball to the hole. He said it was like a child's windup toy, one where if you pulled the string and let go, it would shoot back into the toy. All he had to do was let go of the ball and the string would pull it into the hole.

Another student saw blades of grass growing toward the hole, creating a trough. All she had to do was hit the ball and it would follow the trough into the hole. Many have visualized railroad tracks, without the ties, and the ball sitting on top of the rails. Another student saw a series of golf balls in a line, leading directly to the hole. Some people even see different colors of the path—dark green, yellow, white.

Many golfers believe they are practicing visualization by choosing a spot or target and aiming their shot or putt toward that point. However, choosing a target or goal without seeing how you are going to get there is incomplete.

Many amateurs hit putts that end up "below" the hole. This means that the ball broke or curved to the side of the cup that is physically lower than the other. This happens often because golfers aim to a point (for example, "the right edge of the cup") and don't realize that once they hit the ball, it usually begins to break or curve immediately. The common result: the ball will break more than they expected, ending up on the low side of the cup.

In our golf schools, if a student says he or she is aiming at a spot, I ask the student to take the visualization to the next level, by seeing the entire path of the ball to the hole. In doing so, he or she usually starts the path farther outside the original aiming point

instinctively. Thus, when the student putts, he or she hits the ball along the beginning of the path and allows gravity to do the rest, as the ball breaks into the cup.

At times, a path may not appear so easily. This is quite normal. One student named Donna insisted that no matter what she tried, she couldn't see a line or path. As an exercise, I told her to take her putter and "draw" or trace a path along the ground from the ball to the hole. Reluctant at first, she traced a straight line. Then I had her repeat it two more times. Then I asked her to stand back behind the ball and take a fresh look. She responded, "Oh my, I can see the line." A simple exercise such as tracing the path from the ball to the hole will help train your eye to visualize the putt you want. [10]

Even with these exercises, there will be times when you will not "see" a line. This happens to everyone, including the best golfers in the world. However, tour players have caddies who help them along. Most of us golfers act as our own caddies. If you can't see the line, shift your viewpoint. Instead of looking or waiting for the line to appear, ask yourself, "I know the ball has to get from here to there some way; what's one path it could take to get there?" Choose any path—it could be a straight line or a curved one. Whatever comes to mind first is your intuition telling you what to create. Go with it.

As you visualize, your mind communicates two messages to your body on a subconscious level: (1) how to line up your putt (aim) and (2) exactly how to hit the ball (exertion). You no longer have to think about how to align your feet or how much energy is needed to hit the ball to your target. Your visualization practice tells your body what to do automatically.

Once I see my line, I immediately step up to the ball and set my feet. Without any thought about alignment or where I'm pointing, nearly every time my feet set up exactly along the beginning of the path that I visualized. The mind sees the path and transfers that information to your body to create it.

Furthermore, when you visualize the path vividly, your body will automatically know how much exertion is needed to create the putt. When you see the path in your mind's eye, you have also visualized the distance. The mind then transfers that information to your body, allowing it to release the necessary energy to create the shot.

Another even more powerful form of visualization is visualizing the speed of the ball traveling along the path. For example, if you are facing a fast, downhill putt, imagine the ball traveling along the path in a very slow, deliberate pace. As it finally reaches the hole, imagine the ball just teetering on the lip of the cup and, with the final quarter turn, just barely dropping into the cup. By you simply imagining the pace, your body and putting stroke will respond accordingly with little or no conscious effort.

If you tell yourself to hit the ball a certain way, you activate muscles, often resulting in greater tension or grip pressure and a loss of feel. Many people tend to lose their smooth, natural pendulum and experience a jerky stroke. As a result, they tighten up and pull the putt, or stub the ground, or hit it thin.

If a thousand golfers read the same exact putt, they will actually see a thousand different paths. Everyone is different and processes uniquely. Everyone will hit the ball with a different speed and energy; therefore everyone will have a unique path or line to the hole. When you prepare for your shots, you can listen to the opinions of others, but ultimately the only visualization that matters is yours.

Visualization applies to every shot you make, whether it is putting, chipping, or making a full swing. For shots on the fairway, in addition to visualizing the ball's direction and path, you also want to see its trajectory (ball path into the air; where the ball lands; how it bounces, rolls, and stops).

For example, I always ask my students to pinpoint a final destination for the ball. On the putting green, it's in the hole. On the fairway or even the driving range, choose a specific spot for the ball to come to rest.

One student named Adrienne had a very keen ability to visualize. When I asked her to describe a shot to me, this is what she visualized:

> I see this ball taking off at a fifty-five-degree angle toward that tree, going about halfway to my target, hitting its apex, and then curving slightly to the left because of the wind, which is blowing from right to left, landing ten feet short of my target at that little spot of dark green grass, bouncing three times toward the target, then rolling and stopping exactly at the base of the flag, in the hole.

You may laugh at the specific detail of her visualization, but that is exactly how vividly you want to see your shots.

The likelihood of Adrienne hitting the exact shot that she visualized is probably pretty low. So why is visualizing important and useful? When the greatest golfers of all time, such as Jack Nicklaus, Tiger Woods, Nancy Lopez, and Annika Sorenstam, have shot their greatest rounds, the majority of them said afterward that they actually hit only two, maybe three shots exactly like they visualized. That means that the shots that weren't perfect and exact were still very good.

Visualization helps you focus and narrow the range of possibilities of where your shots might go—from a wide-open area to a specific area or small circle surrounding your desired target, usually about the size of a green or the middle of the fairway.

Step 3—Trusting and committing to your visualization 100 percent

After you visualize the path, you must trust and commit to it 100 percent. Once professional golfers determine their path, they step up with total commitment to create that shot. If there is any doubt or uncertainty, they will often step back and start the process over again, until they have total trust and confidence.

If at any time you begin to lose trust or become uncertain, that negative feeling will cause you to tense up. This tension usually manifests in your dominant hand, causing the putter to turn slightly, often resulting in a pull. If you begin to lose trust or commitment to your path, step back and start your process over. You will always make a better putt.

Susan often walked up to a putt after visualizing the path with confidence. However, after she addressed the ball, she tended to look back and forth between the hole and her feet several times, each time shuffling her feet and adjusting her alignment.

I asked her what she was thinking about as she set up for putts. She said that after seeing the path, she felt confident, but once she addressed the ball, she could no longer see the line and lost that confidence. Accordingly, she would desperately look for the path, with each glance often seeing a completely different one. She doubted her line and herself.

The power of visualization is that once you see the path in your mind, it will always be there, even if you move. It's etched into your mind. Once you step up to the ball, the path is still there, whether you look again or not. A good exercise is to visualize the line, step up immediately to the ball, not look at the hole again, and just let it go. This will help you build trust and commitment to your visualization. I had Susan do this a few times, and she realized that her alignment and putts matched her visualization almost exactly when she trusted it 100 percent.

Sometimes you may follow the visualization process fully, going through each step: (1) knowing what you want, (2) seeing the path, and (3) trusting the path 100 percent, and yet you still might miss the putt. This does not necessarily mean you made a poor putt.

If you allow yourself to hit the shot you envisioned, that's a great shot, regardless of outcome. Golf is not an exact science. Grass is imperfect. The environment is not a vacuum. Uneven surfaces, grains of sand, pebbles, or other particles will regularly kick your ball off line. If you hit the shot the way you wanted to, you have made a good shot. The outcome is out of your hands, and you must let gravity and nature take care of the rest.

It is important to detach from the outcome. The quality of your shot is measured by how well you play the shot, not whether it goes in the hole. This is very difficult for most people to comprehend, given that in Western society nearly everything is measured by outcome.

One student named Mark was a very successful salesperson, always ranked in the top 5 percent of his company. He approached golf with a similar "go get 'em" philosophy. It was very difficult for him to detach from the outcome. If he wasn't shooting better than 95 percent of all golfers, he wasn't happy.

I offered a sales analogy: "Sometimes you may deliver the perfect sales pitch, offer the prospective client exactly what he or she needs, and clearly have a superior product to the competition. But in the end, the client may still choose someone else. To the outsider, you have failed. However, you know inside that you did exactly what you wanted to do to get the sale, and if you had to do it all over again, you would do the same things." He began to see the connection.

I described the parallel to golf. "Imagine you are one hundred twenty-five yards from the hole. You want the ball to end up in the hole, and you visualize a beautiful shot rising high into the air, landing at a specific spot fifteen feet short of the pin, bouncing twice, and rolling into the cup. As soon as you strike the ball, you know inside that it's going in the hole. You watch the ball follow your path exactly as you visualized it. But instead of landing at that spot, bouncing twice and rolling into the hole, the ball lands on the sprinkler head that you didn't see, skips over the green, and goes out of bounds."

"Is this a good shot?" I asked. He thought about it.

"Yes," he said.

"Why?"

"Because I hit the exact shot I wanted."

"Exactly," I said. "The rest is out of your control. In this situation, outcome did not determine the quality of your shot."

John, a sophisticated farmer and self-proclaimed perfectionist, expressed his frustration at his inability to control every shot. In fact, if his ball ended up more than five feet from his target 150 yards away, he was visibly upset. At one point he said, "I can control what happens on the farm, why can't I control every shot on the golf course?"

I responded, "As a farmer, you do your homework to determine the best time to plant your crop, decide when to harvest to achieve a maximum yield, and consider the timing of the market so that you reap higher prices. Sometimes you do everything exactly the way you want to, but Mother Nature ultimately decides the outcome. Looking back on situations like these, if you had to go back and do it again, would you do the same exact thing?"

He nodded and said, "Definitely."

"Why?" I asked.

"Because I know I did everything I wanted to do. I can't control what comes out of the sky."

He smiled.

Trust the process. If you do exactly what you want to do, then you've made a good shot, regardless of the outcome. By detaching from the outcome, you begin to trust yourself and your golf swing. The beauty is that once you begin to detach from the outcome, the outcome will take care of itself. You will begin to hit better shots, shoot lower scores, and surely have more fun.

•••

Visualizing the exact path is important. It will subconsciously tell you how to align your body to create the shot you want. Oftentimes, when we aim shots toward our target, we neglect the slope of the fairway or green, the wind, and our individual ball path (whether we hit a draw or fade) in determining how the ball will land, bounce, and roll. As a result, we often hit solid shots, only to see them end up left or right of our target. By visualizing the exact path, from start to finish, you will automatically tell your body to align itself toward the beginning of the path, taking into account how the ball will travel to your target.

By seeing the path completely, you empower yourself to create that shot. If you are able to visualize the path, then you are more likely to create the shot you desire. If you can't picture it in your

mind, the likelihood of accomplishing it is diminished. Choose a target and visualize the exact path you want the ball to follow—ball path, the curvature of the shot, landing at an exact spot on the ground, bouncing an exact number of times, and rolling to your target. [11] Now hit your shot. Even if you do not hit your target exactly, you will most likely end up in the general direction of your goal.

If you find visualization challenging or difficult, you may want to practice these exercises. With your hand, roll a few golf balls on the putting green and watch how they move toward the hole. Notice how the ball curves, its speed, how it responds to the slope of the green. Do the same on the driving range, tossing a few golf balls into the range and watching them take flight and land. This will help you "see" the path and begin to visualize your shots.

Watching golf on TV is another way to improve your visualization skills. Imagine your golf ball creating a "smoking" trail, similar to skywriting planes, from your starting point to finish. Mentally draw a line with a paintbrush or chalk, either on the putting green or on the fairway.

Visualization applies to every shot you take, whether it is a putt, chip, pitch, or full swing. Jack Nicklaus is one of the greatest players of all time. It is no surprise that he is a master of visualization. His ability to "see" shots in his mind, with great detail and precision, is unparalleled. He not only visualizes the end point, but the exact path, trajectory, how the ball landed, bounced, and rolled to its final destination. Because he has such a keen ability to visualize, he can remember shots that he took over forty years ago.

The following is an excerpt from the article "Play by Pictures: Hit the Shots You Want by 'Seeing' Them First" written by Jack Nicklaus with Ken Bowden, in the July 2000 issue of *Golf Magazine:*

> For some 40 years now, I've gone through the same visualization process before every competitive shot. No other discipline has helped me more, and I'd like to share the process with you here. If your shot execution tends to be careless and inconsistent, visualizing exactly what you want to achieve before setting up and swinging will greatly improve your play.
>
> The more deeply you ingrain what I like to call my "going-to-the-movies" discipline, the more effective you will become at hitting the shots you want to hit. Applying it on the practice tee as well as on the golf course will speed up your mastery of the process. Try this:
>
> First, "see" in your mind's eye where you want the ball to finish. Be realistic about your capabilities, but always imagine positive results, never mis-hits.
>
> Second, "see" the ball flying to the target you've just visualized, to the point of picturing the trajectory, curvature, and roll.

Third, "see" yourself setting up and swinging in such a way as to turn these imaginary pictures into reality.

Fourth, select the club that the completed "movie" tells you is the right one.

If you can complete this or a similar process before you execute your shots, you'll enjoy better, more consistent performance.

EXERCISES

1. Determine what you want. On the putting green, say to yourself, "I want the ball in the hole." On the tee, say, "I want the ball to end up at that patch of grass in the fairway."

2. Visualize the path you want the ball to take. Stand behind the ball, with your target in view, and imagine the ball taking flight along the exact path you want it to follow (for putting, visualize the path along the ground). Notice the trajectory, curve, hang time, landing spot, number of bounces, amount of roll, and stopping point (all the way into the hole for both putts and regular shots). When you visualize, consider the wind, your desired ball flight (draw, fade, or straight), and how the ball will bounce and roll. If you are putting and there is a slope on the green, imagine the exact path you want the ball to follow into the hole, including the break and speed caused by the slope. Choose the exact spot of the cup at which you want the ball to enter the hole.

3. TRUST and COMMIT to your visualization 100 percent, and set up to the ball immediately. When you visualize, your mind tells your body exactly what to do—how to align itself and how much exertion is needed to hit the ball into the hole. If you have any doubt or uncertainty, those negative thoughts will manifest into tension and affect the quality of your shot. Trust and commit fully and you will always make a better shot.

4. Let go. Allow your body to make the shot you visualized.

>>>>

12

5. On the putting green, hit a set of five putts from the north at the following distances: one foot, two feet, three feet, four feet, and five feet [12]. Then hit sets of five putts from the south, east, and west sides of the same hole. On the last set of putts, follow the same process: determine what you want, visualize the path, and then, before putting the ball, close your eyes and putt with your eyes closed. This is where the real trust begins.

VISUALIZE THE SHOT OFF THE GOLF COURSE

Know what you want
Believe in what you want
See it happen

While peak performance is often a goal for professional athletes, artists, and musicians, I believe all people share a similar desire for personal achievement in their lives. However, fear of failure, disappointment, and frustration often preempt these desires from manifesting.

Adopt a regular practice of acknowledging your wants and desires. This simple shift in how you view your life will begin an enlightening process, opening you to a world of endless possibilities. If you are unable to imagine what you want in your life, you will most likely never realize it. Similarly, if you expect the worst, you can be certain that it will come to pass. Whatever we put our energy and focus on is destined to manifest.

One of our most powerful tools as living creatures is visualization. It can have a tremendous impact on how we live. Ask yourself what you want in all aspects of your life—financially, emotionally, physically, and spiritually. Visualize it in your mind's eye and then trust and commit to it, allowing it to manifest.

My wife is a writer and also teaches creative writing classes. Many of her students experience writer's block, or the inability to allow their ideas and creativity to flow freely from mind to paper. Like her students, many of us experience a form of writer's block in our daily lives. We prevent our creative mind from flourishing and often block out thoughts of our true wants and desires, on both conscious and subconscious levels.

Dave took a private lesson with me to help him lower his handicap. He knew he could hit the ball well, but he just could not seem to score well. After analyzing his game and his mind-set, I noticed that even though he had the ability to hit any type of shot, rarely did he know exactly what kind of shot he wanted.

There was little creativity to his game. He was regimented in his approach to golf. Robotic and stiff, he measured every shot to the last quarter inch and then automatically selected a club that matched that distance. I asked him if he ever used his imagination to create different types of shots from the same distance. He looked confused.

I asked him if he could remember a time when he used his imagination as a child. He told me that when he was young, he was very creative, and drawing was his favorite thing to do. I asked him if he still drew. He said he gradually gave up his artistic interest as his parents and teachers offered little support and, at times, discouraged such pursuits in lieu of traditional education. As a result, he pushed away a part of himself. He noticed that his life choices, as well as his golf game, followed a similar pattern. He chose a career path that was not his true passion, but rather the safe and traditional route. Likewise, his golf game was mechanical, almost programmed.

I told him to start using his imagination and visualize what he wanted. I shared with him a great tool to explore and visualize what he wanted in life. My wife uses this in her classes. She gives her students fifteen minutes to flip through as many magazines as possible, tearing out pages that catch their attention. No thoughts, no commentary, and no censorship allowed. This free-flowing exercise allows the subconscious to take over. After fifteen minutes of tearing, the students then begin to cut and paste. On one five-by-seven-inch card, they arrange pictures, words, and symbols in any design. This collage usually turns out to be a representation of each person's vision of what he or she wants in life.

Most people frame this collage and display it as a daily reminder of what they desire. This exercise is a great way to give you an opportunity to explore and discover what you want and put it into a concrete, tangible form. This five-by-seven-inch collage becomes a powerful tool to visualize your desires, the first step toward creating the life you want.

Dave did this exercise, and it led him back to his passion for drawing once again. He still struggled with self-imposed limitations. However, whenever he felt like he had "writer's block," he looked at his collage and it inspired him to move forward. He also changed how he played the game of golf. He discovered a whole new approach. His creativity for shots flowed, and not only did he enjoy the game more, but his scores also improved beyond what he could ever have imagined.

•••

1. KNOW WHAT YOU WANT. How often do you ask yourself, "What do I really want?" Probably not often enough. Throughout the day, continually ask yourself what you want. Begin with basic desires such as "I'm hungry, I want a chocolate chip cookie" or "I'm tired, I want to close my eyes and sleep." Gradually, you will begin to ask yourself the question more often. The practice of asking yourself what you want will help you explore your true desires in life. Explore what you want in your life on all levels: financially, romantically, physically, emotionally, and spiritually. There are no limits. What do *you* want?

》》》

2. BELIEVE IN WHAT YOU WANT. Visualizing your desires sets the stage. Truly believing in them helps them become a reality. Picture yourself living in a world with all your wants and desires. If you have faith that your deepest wants and desires are real, they will begin to manifest for you.

3. SEE IT HAPPEN. A powerful way to "see" it happen in everyday life is to write it down. The act of writing down your desires is a powerful exercise. It helps bring your ideas, hopes, and dreams into a conscious, physical existence. Write them down in a journal, on a white board, or on a small piece of paper you carry in your wallet. If it has to do with your golf game, place the piece of paper in your golf bag, where it will remind you of your goals and inspire you to see them through. You can also use pictures or create a collage that represents your visualization. Display it visibly so that you can see it every day.

CREATE YOUR OWN PRE-SHOT RITUAL

"When I play my best golf, I feel as if I'm in a fog, standing back watching the earth in orbit with a golf club in my hands."

Mickey Wright

MOST golfers are familiar with what's called the "pre-shot routine." In fact, many of you probably have one, without even realizing it. In our clinics and programs, we always have our clients fill out an intake survey, and we find out if they use a pre-shot routine. Approximately 15 percent of our students claim they use one regularly, while 35 percent say they use one but not consistently. Some 35 percent are unaware if they use one or not, and the remaining 15 percent say they definitely do not.

The pre-shot routine is a critical part of the game and, at times, it may be even more important than the golf swing itself. It is a series of the same actions or movements that a golfer makes before every shot. For example, every time Fred Couples gets ready to hit, he lifts up his arm to loosen his shirtsleeve, lines up the shot, sets up to the ball, and swings. He repeats this same routine before every shot.

The pre-shot routine is designed to help golfers enter a state of peak performance. Once you begin your routine, you subconsciously tell yourself that the golf shot is coming. When the routine begins, golfers are telling themselves, "It's time to focus and hit the shot I want."

Routines are helpful in that they improve our efficiency and elevate our performance. However, routines are often just a rote series of activities that are mundane or insignificant. To be truly beneficial, a pre-shot routine must take on greater significance and meaning. It can elevate you to a higher level of performance if it is completed with intention and purpose. If a pre-shot routine takes on such meaning, then it is no longer a simple, repeated series of actions. It is a *ritual*.

Rituals have a historical and ancient purpose. According to Barbara Bizou, author of *The Joy of Ritual*, "The word ritual derives from an Indo-European root meaning 'to fit together.' It is literally an act where we join the metaphysical with the physical as a means of calling spirit into our material lives. Rituals remind us that we have the power to design our own lives." Rituals have been known to help individuals achieve a higher state of being or consciousness and even transformation.

Most people practice rituals in their daily lives, without realizing it. It may be working out or exercising first thing in the morning or sitting quietly with a book at the end of the day. Many people have rituals when they arrive at work, perhaps setting goals, organizing their desk, and listing their tasks for the day. Families and couples practice rituals such as having dinner together at a certain time of the day or going on an annual vacation.

Many professional athletes, as well as artists and performing artists, use rituals to prepare themselves for their "work." For example, when Andre Agassi prepares for a serve, he has his own pre-serve ritual. He stands at a particular place on the baseline, chooses one ball to serve, bounces it a set number of times, pauses, tosses the ball in the air, and hits the serve. It is exactly the same ritual for each and every serve. In basketball, when a player attempts a free throw, he or she uses a consistent pre-shot ritual with the same bounces, rhythm, and timing before every shot.

A ritual creates consistency and increases focus and concentration, eliminating all distractions. There are two types of distractions in the world—external and internal. External distractions are noises or talking, people or items in motion catching your eye, or perhaps a bee landing on your golf ball. Over time, and with practice, you can almost ignore external distractions and let them flow around you.

Internal distractions are more difficult to ignore. This is how you feel inside and the chatter in your mind—the inner voice thinking about anything and everything, including:

- the pressure of making a putt to shoot your personal best score or win a match or skins game
- worry about slowing down others
- fear of failure
- embarrassment
- self-criticism
- dwelling over prior shots
- concern about negative outcomes
- doubt
- thinking about non-golf issues such as work or family

A consistent pre-shot ritual will help eliminate all distractions, external and internal, and increase your level of performance, whether in golf, work, or any other activity.

Susan was an intelligent, articulate professional with an impressive career in investment banking. She was a self-proclaimed numbers person who calculated everything she did, from work to home life to sports. She excelled in everything she attempted. She had the potential to be a fine golfer but had a hard time relaxing and letting it flow.

After working with her for a few minutes, I noticed that she seemed very uncomfortable and rigid as she approached each shot.

I asked her, "What do you think about when you are preparing for a shot?"

She replied, "Well, I'm trying to make sure everything is in the right place. In other words, that my grip is correct and that my left elbow is straight. I remember that from a beginning golf lesson. I try to keep my head down. I make my feet line up to the direction of my shot and I also check that my feet are shoulder width apart. I try to keep my knees bent a little. Then I try to move the club back along an imaginary line and stop the club so that it doesn't go too far back . . ."

The checklist went on and on and on. Susan had so many things to remember that by the time she swung the club, she was rigid and tight. She suffered from information overload or analysis paralysis —attempting to process too much information at the same time, causing her body to shut down.

Most physical activities, including the golf swing, can be natural and flowing when mental interference is minimized. Take walking, for example. Do you think about *how* to walk? In other words, when you walk, do you think to yourself, "OK, I need to put my right foot down twelve inches ahead of my left foot and at the same time swing my left arm to help me maintain my balance. Next I need to shift weight from my left foot to my right foot and move my left foot ahead of my right and swing my right arm at the same time."

No, you just do it. If you tried to tell yourself how to walk, you wouldn't be able to move very far. Watch a baby learning to walk. He or she just moves one foot in front of the other and eventually figures out what to do—no real coaching necessary. For Susan and many other golfers, the mind needs to quiet down in order for the body to serve its function. The pre-shot ritual will do exactly that.

Pre-shot rituals are extremely important in golf for many other reasons. A ritual separates the physical act of golfing (swinging and hitting the ball) from just being on the golf course. As mentioned earlier, a typical round of golf lasts four hours, but you actually play golf or hit shots for only three minutes! What are you doing during the three hours and fifty-seven minutes of downtime?

You're doing a lot of things: walking, looking for your golf ball, lining up putts, waiting for others to play, and hopefully having fun and enjoying the company. However, you may also be engaging in self-talk and self-criticism: attempting to figure out what's wrong with your swing, thinking about your score, worrying about work or your family. A ritual can separate "playing golf" from "being on the golf course."

It is important to personalize a ritual. The actions, timing, and rhythm of your ritual will be different from everyone else's. Experiment and find what works best. Some people have one pre-shot ritual on the putting green and another for fairway shots. The key is to create a pre-shot ritual that will be consistent before each and every shot, to eliminate distractions and help you focus and concentrate.

Watch the best golfers in the world at a tournament or on TV. They are relentless about their pre-shot rituals. Tiger Woods, Jim Furyk, Jack Nicklaus, Arnold Palmer, Annika Sorenstam, and Karrie Webb have their own unique rituals that they repeat consistently before every shot.

Rituals help golfers increase their focus and concentration instantaneously. The key to a pre-shot ritual is the beginning. I recommend using a physical "cue" or "trigger" at the beginning of your ritual. It's like when you flip on a light switch. What happens? The light turns on. Your cue is like a light switch, telling your mind and body that you are starting your shot. Your level of concentration and focus will increase immediately.

When selecting a cue, choose one that you may already use naturally. Most people aren't aware that they already have a cue and pre-shot ritual. Observe what you do before every shot. Notice if you start each pre-shot ritual with the same movement.

Cues can be anything: holding the club in a particular hand, leaning on your club, plumb-bobbing, crouching down, tugging a

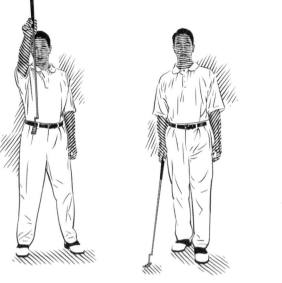

sleeve, tipping a hat, fixing your sunglasses, or touching your belt buckle. [13] I hold the club in my right hand and place it down on the ground in front of me—that's my cue.

This trigger or cue is the equivalent to the starting gun at a track meet. Top athletes in these sports train their bodies to respond reflexively to the sound of the gun. The gun goes off and their body responds. They don't think.

•••

Many golfers tend to rush their shots. I've heard many different reasons for rushing from my clients:

- ••• "I want to get it over as quickly as possible."
- ••• "I'm worried about slowing people down."
- ••• "I don't want the group behind us to catch up and watch me."
- ••• "I want to hit the shot quickly before I start thinking about it."

14

These kinds of thoughts build tension and anxiety, leading to poor performance.

I often watch golfers walking off the 18th green. They look listless and pale, dragging their feet toward the clubhouse. It's as if they haven't taken a breath in four hours. Notice how golfers often hold their breath as they prepare for a shot. It hinders their performance.

Combine the cue in your pre-shot ritual with a deep breath. Breathing will do two things for you: (1) slow you down and help you relax, and (2) provide your body with the energy necessary to create the shot you want. Energize your body by getting the necessary oxygen to your muscles, while clearing your mind to perform at your optimum.

There are many effective breathing techniques that will help you relax and perform at a higher level. One technique that I like is called the four-part breath: (1) inhale for five seconds, (2) rest for five seconds, (3) exhale for five seconds, and (4) rest for five seconds. As you exhale and rest, feel yourself relaxing and "sinking" into your

body. This will help you clear out all thoughts and focus on your shot. You may also choose to incorporate at least one more deep breath into your pre-shot ritual, perhaps just prior to your shot.

As I exhale, I feel myself settling into my body, especially into my legs. Visualize a cloud, bubble, or fog surrounding you, the ball, the target, and the entire area leading up to the hole. This will elevate your level of focus and concentration by placing you within a specific playing space. Oftentimes you'll see professional golfers put their hands on each side of their hat, blocking out peripheral distractions. By creating tunnel vision, they focus on the shot they want to create.

Golfers of all abilities, from pure beginners to seasoned professionals, can benefit by using a pre-shot ritual *for every shot.* A ritual can be simple: taking a deep breath, visualizing a path, walking up to the ball, pausing, and letting it go. [14] For others, it may be a bit more involved, incorporating practice swings. Others will include as part of their ritual reminders to make sure that they are balanced and have a light grip.

Some golfers fear that if they use a ritual, they will slow down play. The ritual need not be complicated or long—just meaningful. If a golfer takes time to follow a consistent pre-shot ritual, he or she will hit better shots with greater consistency. This will therefore save time overall, as it will minimize errant shots, which create the need for even more swings.

Joe showed me his pre-shot ritual on the putting green. I timed it on my watch, and it took approximately two minutes for every shot. He included all sorts of motions and movements, even checking to make sure his shirt was tucked in straight. It was so complicated that by the time he hit the putt, he had lost his concentration. He was more focused on all the parts leading up to the shot than on the shot itself.

I asked him to simplify the pre-shot ritual to its bare necessities. He cut out unnecessary movements that did not flow naturally or help his concentration. At the same time he added a deep breath to slow him down. The idea is to create a pre-shot ritual that is simple and triggers your body into a state of peak performance.

The number one complaint among golfers is inconsistency. One shot may be perfectly straight down the middle of the fairway to your target, while the next is a shank into the woods. If you can be consistent in your pre-shot ritual before every shot, you will increase the consistency in your ball-striking.

During a round of golf, you will hit a poor shot every now and then. In fact, players at the highest level, including Tiger Woods and Annika Sorenstam, will hit errant shots. The key to their success is that they let go of those poor shots. Once they start their pre-shot ritual, the prior shot is all but forgotten.

On the other hand, many amateurs respond emotionally, allowing their anger and frustration to negatively affect their future play. Each successive shot is hampered by memories of a prior shot.

I had a playing lesson with Ian, who was a member of the high school golf team. He had a solid overall game but would often dwell on his poor shots. A typical series of shots would be as follows: a pulled tee shot, followed by a difficult fairway wood from the rough, followed by an angry mid-iron, followed by a poor shot from a green-side bunker, a fat chip shot, and then multiple putts in frustration. He rushed from shot to shot, without pausing to start fresh.

Every golfer has experienced something similar to this, professionals and amateurs alike. How can you work through these times? Practice and learn to trust your pre-shot ritual. It is designed to reset you for a new beginning. Regardless of prior experiences, a well-intended, purposeful ritual will set you up for success on the next shot. You will experience rejuvenation with every shot.

It is also important not to dwell on good shots. How many times do you follow a birdie with a poor tee shot or a double bogey? Often, you're still thinking about the last shot or hole, which distracts you from the present shot. Your pre-shot ritual with help you hit your shots with a blank slate.

The process of a pre-shot ritual communicates an essential message to yourself: (1) now is the moment to focus on your shot, and (2) all that exists is me, the ball, and the hole. The pre-shot ritual clears your mind of distractions, such as thoughts of poor shots, inner commentary about faults in your swing, second-guessing shots, or extraneous thoughts about life off the golf course (work, family, money).

Using a cue to start your pre-shot ritual will separate "playing" golf from the "experience" of being on the golf course. This process will save you from a disastrous hole or series of disastrous holes. The pre-shot ritual will always set you up for the opportunity to hit a successful shot.

Creating a pre-shot ritual that consists of significant actions, thoughts, or cues will help you achieve a higher level of consistency in all of your golf shots. Consistently using a pre-shot ritual on the golf course is a challenge. Golfers seem to rush from shot to shot, rarely pausing or slowing down. The ritual will help you slow down your thoughts and focus on the shot at hand. Rituals that have a consistent flow will help you develop a rhythm that will increase your concentration and create the shots you want.

Remember, your pre-shot ritual is meaningful to you and that's all that matters. Do what feels right. If your pre-shot ritual settles you down and allows you to create the best shot possible, then it is worth the investment.

When you are in the middle of a round, and you are distracted by others or you are not playing as well as you wish, the pre-shot ritual becomes essential to your game. It brings you back to the present and allows you to play your best golf. Every time you start your ritual, you are in a sense resetting your internal clock. It is always a fresh beginning.

Fran had a very nice golf game when she could forget about everyone else and start focusing on her own experience. Her self-proclaimed challenge was to stop taking care of everyone except herself. She was always the caretaker, making sure that her playing partners moved along and that the other golfers behind them weren't waiting. She constantly looked over her shoulder, and even if it was clear, she worried that the group behind would drive up and complain that she was slow.

So when it came to her shot, she literally hit the ball while in motion, without even pausing to establish her feet. She was so concerned about everyone else that she forgot about herself.

Golf is a game in which you are alone and not alone at the same time. You hit your shots individually, but you are playing along with three others in your group, as well as dozens of others on the golf course. You can't control other golfers. All you can do is focus on yourself and your shot.

If the group behind you is playing faster than your group, do what you need to do to keep up, even if you have to run between shots. However, once it's your shot, that's your time. Start your pre-shot ritual and slow down to your regular, consistent pace.

On the other hand, you may be stuck in a slow six-hour round and have to wait for the group in front of you on every shot. When it's finally your shot, start your pre-shot ritual and follow that same, natural rhythm and pace for all your shots.

Regardless of what is happening around you, you can always maintain consistency in your game with the pre-shot ritual. This is what I call "finding the peace amidst the chaos."

EXERCISES

1. Select a cue or trigger to start your pre-shot ritual. Notice what you do naturally as you prepare to make a shot. It can be anything, as long as you do it consistently for every shot. Examples of cues or triggers include: holding the club in one hand and deliberately placing it on the ground; crouching down; plumb-bobbing; tugging a sleeve; tipping a cap; or pointing the club toward your target.

2. Take a deep breath simultaneously with your cue or trigger. Taking a deep breath slows you down, relaxes your body and mind, and energizes you to create the shot you want. One breathing technique that is very effective is the four-part breath. Inhale deeply into the abdomen for several seconds, rest for several seconds, exhale for several seconds, rest for several seconds, and repeat. When you inhale, your stomach should rise, which indicates that you have fully utilized your lung capacity.

3. Customize your ritual. Do what feels right and natural. Begin with your trigger and a deep breath. After that it's up to you. The key is to keep the ritual consistent for every shot. The timing and rhythm of your ritual is as important as what you do. If at any time you are interrupted during your pre-shot ritual, start again. You will have better concentration and make a better shot. Imagine videotaping your pre-shot ritual before every shot and watching after the round. You would want it to feel as if you were watching the same process over and over again. Once you start your pre-shot ritual, you are telling your body, "Now I am starting my shot," which will increase your focus and concentration and help you perform at a higher level.

》》》

4. Combine the fourth with the first three Principles of Golf to make a pre-shot ritual. For example:

    a. Start the pre-shot ritual with your cue or trigger and breathe deeply into your abdomen *(The Fourth Principle—Pre-shot Ritual)*.

    b. Determine what you want and visualize the shot you desire *(The Third Principle—Visualize the Shot)*.

    c. Set up to the ball and find your perfect balance, planting your feet into the ground *(The First Principle—Get Grounded)*.

    d. Relax your hands and connect with the club *(The Second Principle—Develop Feel)*.

    e. Let your swing flow naturally from the pre-shot ritual into a perfect golf shot.

CREATE YOUR OWN
PRE-SHOT RITUAL
OFF THE GOLF COURSE

Create a personal ritual
Find your own space
Honor your ritual daily

Most of us follow a daily schedule. However, it consists of nothing more than a series of monotonous, rote activities. We wake up, brush our teeth, get ready to go to work, have breakfast, drive to the office, etc. The routine is mundane.

Andy was an accountant who followed a very strict daily routine at work and in life. To his detriment, his routine was driven by the "shoulds." In other words, his routine consisted of what he felt he should do, rather than what he wanted to do. He rarely included time for himself in his daily routine.

When I suggested that he find time for himself, he immediately resisted. "I don't have time for myself. Every minute of every day is spent on my job or my family, and if I have free time, I'm running errands or fixing something in the house. I can't allow myself the luxury of doing something that I want to do."

This is a very common response from many of my clients. Yes, we are all living lives that are very complex. However, if we step back and take a moment to reflect and look at the big picture, we often realize that we may be able to achieve a better way of life with very little effort. A few moments of simplicity can add a level of depth and meaning to our routines, transforming them into rituals.

Creating meaningful rituals will add awareness and meaning to your daily life. Choose activities or cues that will remind you of your deeper existence. Meditation is a very popular form of ritual. It can be as simple as sitting in silence and focusing on your breath for five minutes, or as formal as sitting zazen for a weeklong meditation retreat. With practice, meditation can take as little as ten seconds. When feeling stressed, I simply close my eyes, take a deep breath, and visualize myself in a state of total relaxation on a white, sandy beach. I immediately begin to relax.

For Andy, working out was always a great form of relaxation. His challenge was finding the time. After analyzing his typical daily schedule, he decided that instead of spending his lunchtime at a restaurant, he would work out and eat lunch at his desk. He looked forward to this time for himself and made it a part of his daily ritual. As a result, his level of stress decreased and his productivity at work improved. In his personal life, he discovered calm and patience that he had never had before. As a result, all of his relationships improved and he felt he was a better husband and father.

Practice your ritual at the same time every day, and you will begin to discover how you can create an environment that helps you enter a place of higher focus and concentration. Regular rituals will lead you to a place where feelings of tranquillity and peace always exist, even in times of duress and chaos. Your ritual will provide you with a sacred space for relaxation and contemplation.

•••

1. CREATE A PERSONAL RITUAL. Develop a meaningful ritual that fits best with your lifestyle. Some work out, practice meditation, or do yoga every morning. Others take walks in nature or read a motivational quote to help them shift to a deeper, more contemplative state. With a ritual, you will find it easier to achieve a higher level of personal reflection in your daily life.

》》》

2. FIND YOUR OWN SPACE. Many of us live with other people—roommates, spouses, partners, families. Finding your own space can sometimes be difficult. Having moved several times over the past few decades, from large spaces to small spaces and back again, I've discovered a way to find and keep my own space. I do this by building an altar, which consists of a small area somewhere in the house that has a small table or stand where I can place items of special meaning to me. Everyone has special objects that carry some sort of significance in their lives. On my altar, I have a few sculptures and carvings from my travels and some precious stones and gems that offer me inspiration. I also have my scorecard from the first time I broke 80, and a golf ball Nick Faldo tossed into the crowd after shooting an eagle on the 10th hole at Riviera Country Club during the 1989 Los Angeles Open. Gather items of this nature and build your own altar. It need not be complicated or religious in nature—think of it as a place of your own that honors and reminds you of what you love. You can always go to your altar when you need inspiration or guidance.

3. HONOR YOUR RITUAL DAILY. Regularity and consistency in your ritual will help you achieve a deeper state of relaxation. Select a specific time and place. Beware of distractions. Agree in advance to let the answering machine pick up. During your walk, avoid running errands. After you establish a daily practice, you will find it becomes very easy to enter a deeper, more peaceful state of existence not only during your ritual, but also throughout your day, no matter where you are or what you are doing.

FIND YOUR
NATURAL SWING

"People are always telling me I should do one thing or another. I should change my grip or shorten my swing. I should practice more and goof around less. I shouldn't smile on Sunday . . . I should . . . I shouldn't . . . Frankly I don't know why they worry. It's my life—and I don't worry."

Fred Couples

TODAY'S modern era of golf instruction has reached an unprecedented level. New golf gadgets and swing aids are invented every day to help people along on their pursuit of the perfect golf swing. Swing doctors and golf gurus, with techniques ranging from the traditional to the revolutionary, have inundated the golfing world. With such a prolific presence of golf-related tools and methodologies, at times it can be extremely confusing for the average golfer. Which way is right or best?

John was one of the most schooled students I had ever worked with. Over the years, he had seen close to fifteen different golf instructors, ranging from the unknown at the local driving range to some of the most famous celebrity golf gurus in the country. He said that with each different instructor, he had learned something new. However, some of the methods contradicted each other, and he often ended up confused and frustrated as to which school of thought was correct. He visited me to help him sort out his confusion.

I explained to John that not all swings are the same. No two people are alike; no two swings are alike. Everyone has a unique body type, physical ability, mental strength, and personal style. The key is to find your own natural swing, one that fits you and leverages your strengths. I believe in one "perfect" swing. That is, one perfect and *unique* swing for each and every person.

I like to think of Fred Astaire when it comes to the natural swing.

In the film *Carefree*, a scene takes place on a driving range in which Fred is hitting golf balls as his friends look on. Ginger Rogers offers him the greatest of challenges: Can you dance and hit golf balls at the same time?

The music starts and Fred begins to dance. In the middle of his number, you see five golf balls teed up in a row. He grabs a driver and hits all five golf balls in succession, without missing a beat. You can see each golf ball following the same exact path to the same target. He moves with such ease and fluidity, always smiling and gliding on his feet. It is clear that Fred Astaire put his personality and individual style into creating his *own natural swing*.

Arnold Palmer puts his spirit and personality not only into his golf swing, but into his entire approach to golf. He walks, swings, and competes with nothing less than pure passion and competitive fire. He is himself through and through, on and off the golf course. His swing is as unique as his personality. Arnold Palmer's natural swing is perfect for him and him alone.

Jim Furyk, the 2003 U.S. Open champion, has what is considered to be one of the most unorthodox swings in the world. It has an unusual looping motion that most conventional swing methods would not recommend. He has tried to change it, only to find that a more conventional swing felt unnatural, foreign, and unreliable, especially in difficult competitive situations. When he returned to his own natural swing, he felt more confident and comfortable. He developed total confidence in his swing, especially in pressure-filled situations which allowed him to swing freely and win the U.S. Open in record-setting fashion.

Copying or emulating others' golf swings may help you develop some good habits. However, finding your own natural swing, one that you can trust and embrace, will be liberating and, more importantly, enduring. Play the way you are meant to play, with your own style and personality.

I coached one golfer named Phil who was extremely athletic and participated in all types of sports and activities, including basketball, football, yoga, weights, and running. He was strong yet flexible, and he had the physique and coordination that would warrant a solid golf swing.

I observed him warming up on the driving range and noticed that he seemed very uncomfortable. He was attempting to guide the golf club slowly and deliberately. Each time, he would set up to the ball, stare at it for at least fifteen seconds, and start a slow, smooth backswing. Just as he was about to begin his downswing, he would tense up and swing the club as hard as he could. He connected on one out of every fifteen swings, but more often than not he missed the ball entirely.

I knew Phil enjoyed playing basketball, so I offered an analogy that might help him with his golf swing.

I asked him, "If you were playing basketball and had a breakaway layup, would you go in for a high-flying slam dunk or a gentle, fingertip roll over the rim?"

He replied, "Definitely the jam!"

"There's the answer to your golf swing," I said.

He looked extremely confused now. I told him that his natural tendency as an athlete is to be commanding. However, he was trying to swing a golf club in just the opposite fashion, slow and deliberate.

He wasn't going with his instincts or trusting his natural swing. To bring out more of his personality and natural disposition, we developed a more up-tempo rhythm and flow. I had him close his eyes and begin swinging the club in a manner that seemed natural to him. It didn't matter whether it was flat or steep, slow or fast. What was important was that he found the rhythm and timing that was perfect for him.

Eventually, he developed a swing that seemed effortless and natural. It was a powerful swing with a quick tempo. For others, this would have been too fast, but for Phil it was perfect. It fit his personality. He could relate to his swing and channel his natural intensity into how he played golf.

This also applied to his golf course management. When confronted with the option of hitting over a hazard or going around it, he would opt for the more conservative route. However, his instinct always told him to "go for it!" Even though he was playing it safe, he would usually end up hitting a poor shot, because of this inner conflict. With his naturally aggressive style, he began to take a direct line to the hole, matching his zest for risk and reward. He began to experience golf from a new perspective. He played with fire and it felt comfortable and natural.

It would be very strange to see someone like John Daly laying up on a par-5. It's not in his nature. He only knows how to "grip it and rip it." Players like Seve Ballesteros, Raymond Floyd, and Lee Trevino would not be the golfers they are unless they gave it their all on every shot.

On the other hand, it would seem out of place for Ernie Els, Fred Couples, or Tom Kite to swing out of control. Their nature is to swing easy and relaxed. For each and every golfer, there is a perfect way to play.

Bring out your personality and natural disposition in your golf swing. If you are an easygoing, laid-back person, then swing the club in the same fashion. If you tend to be more assertive, then your swing can reflect that as well.

I meet some very nice people in our golf program. At times, some confess that back home they lead very stressful lives. In fact, many tell me about their pressure-filled careers, challenges in their personal lives, and daily feelings of uncertainty and stress.

15

This energy transfers into their golf swings as well. By observing one swing, I can guess how much tension is in that person's life. It often seems as if they are gripping a sledgehammer as tightly as they can, trying to knock down a brick wall. [15]

You can also use your golf swing to work on a part of your personality that you want to change. If you are tense and want to relax, then think of the smooth, easygoing tempo of Ernie Els and Fred Couples. As you approach the ball and swing the club, think in your mind, "easy, smooth, flowing, relaxed." [16] This will certainly help you on the golf course, but more importantly, you can apply this to your life off the golf course as well.

Instead of playing golf in a hurried fashion, take your time. Walk slowly and breathe deeply. Give yourself an entire morning or afternoon to focus on golf and your experience on the golf course, without distractions such as cell phones or pagers.

16

Each of us has a one-of-a-kind existence. Search your soul for that essence and express it on the golf course. It will have a great impact on your game. Instruction manuals, books, magazines, videos, and coaching can only show you different paths. You must find and choose the right one for yourself. Even with the Principles and exercises in this book, take what is useful to you and apply it. Perhaps it is one or two of the Principles, or all seven, and then again, the program may not be the right thing for you at all. That's fine. Find what works for *you*, and you will truly appreciate this game and enjoy it for the long run.

Honor your own way of playing golf.

Harry was seventy-four years old when he took our clinic. He wanted to regain the distance he had lost over the years. After taking our clinic, he began to relax his grip and started hitting the ball straighter and farther. However, he still felt as if he didn't have enough to keep up with the younger players in his golf club.

I asked, "How many fairways do you hit on average during a round of golf?"

He said, "Almost all of them, but they don't go very far."

He was so concerned about one aspect of the game—distance—

that he had forgotten about other aspects that were equally, if not more, important, including accuracy.

Watch a few seniors play golf at your home course. They may tend to hit it shorter than some of the younger players, but they often hit the ball straight down the middle of the fairway. These players know their strengths and play them to their advantage. They string together shots they have the ability and skill to create. Instead of trying to hit a driver 275 yards on a long par-4, which they are not capable of doing, they'll hit two medium-length shots (150–175 yards each), followed by a chip shot and one putt. The result? Par.

Young, high handicappers often step up to the tee and attempt to "kill" the ball with their driver. It usually slices severely into trouble. They feel they must make up for the poor drive by attempting an extremely difficult shot that most professionals wouldn't attempt (such as reaching the green from 245 yards over a lake). They only end up in more trouble.

Julie played in a regular foursome on Tuesdays with three of her best friends. They were all quite good players. However, Julie's friends had very similar styles on the golf course. They had "go for it" attitudes. For example, on a short par-4, all three would always attempt to reach the green with their drivers, even if there were hazards surrounding it. Julie always felt that she should do the same.

However, she had more finesse and style than her friends. I suggested that she play her own game, rather than conforming to what the others were doing. Instead of hitting a driver, which often got her into trouble, perhaps she could hit a fairway wood or mid-iron off the tee and then hit a short iron to the green, leaving her with a greater chance for birdie or par.

Don't conform to what others are doing. If your playing partners hit drivers off the tee, but you are more comfortable hitting a 3-wood or a mid-iron, go for it. Play the way that feels right and matches best with your ability. You'll always make a more confident swing.

Jim complained that his shots, though straight and consistent, would always fly with a low trajectory. Compared to some of his playing partners, he had a much lower ball flight. I asked him if this was affecting his overall play. He responded that he usually played just as well, if not better.

I explained how everyone has his or her own style of play. For example, from fifty yards out, some people hit high shots with a wedge directly to the green, while others like to play a ground game, hitting the bump-and-run along the fairway. It really doesn't matter, as long as you find something that is comfortable and natural for you.

17

One of the best ways to find your natural swing and style of play is to experiment hitting shots from the same spot with different clubs. For example, from seventy-five yards, try hitting every club in your bag. [17] You'll find that you have to be creative with each club.

Or try the opposite: play an entire hole with just one club. Choose your favorite club and use it for every shot from tee to green. You'll get there and may find it more fun than ever. Be creative and imaginative. This will help you when you play your regular game.

Experiment with different swings and styles of play to find the one that is most natural for you.

On the PGA, LPGA, and Champions Tours, no two swings are exactly alike. In fact, it would be difficult to find any two swings in the world that are exactly alike. Be *you* on the golf course. Express yourself through your golf swing.

EXERCISES

1. View the golf swing as a natural and flowing motion. It is a part of who you are. It is an instinctive activity like walking or breathing.

2. Try the following types of swings in practice without hitting golf balls.

   a.   A relaxed swing
   b.   A powerful swing
   c.   A smooth swing
   d.   An assertive swing
   e.   An easy swing
   f.   A happy swing
   g.   A flowing swing

3. Explore other golf swings that reflect how you want to be. For example, if you want to have more fun and enjoyment on the golf course, visualize a swing that exudes positive energy (like Fred Astaire's). Picture yourself smiling or laughing when you're swinging the club. Or if want to be more driven and assertive, channel that level of intensity into your golf swing.

4. Find *your* own natural swing. Like your signature or fingerprint, your swing is unique, one-of-a-kind, and absolutely yours. Experience your golf swing as you never have before. It will feel so easy and natural, it will seem like a part of who you are, and most importantly—it will be your own!

FIND YOUR NATURAL SWING
OFF THE GOLF COURSE

Trust your instincts
Find your own way
Search your soul

We were all born with a divine, creative energy that encourages us to explore our world. We were fascinated by the simplest of things. Somewhere along the way, we may have begun to ignore and doubt that inner spirit. It was pushed aside, and after years of neglect, it seemed to disappear.

I went to college with a guy named Brian, who grew up in a very strict household. He went to private prep schools and his parents always demanded that he follow a traditional pattern, similar to his father, who was a dentist, and his older brothers, one of whom was a doctor and the other an investment banker. Following in the footsteps of his family, he was always at the top of his class, graduated from law school with honors, and passed the bar on his first attempt.

However, all along his path he felt a constant conflict between what he wanted to do and what he felt he had to do. Brian always enjoyed being in front of an audience and making people laugh. He had loved performing in school plays and skits, but gave it up to follow a path that was chosen for him.

As he studied for the bar exam, I could tell he was very sad and depressed. I asked him if it was because of the test or if it was something else. He said that he had absolutely no interest at all in becoming an attorney and that he was doing it for his parents. I asked him, "If you could do anything in your life, right now, what would it be? What is your passion?" He said, "To be an actor."

And with that conversation, he found his own natural swing and the path to his true passion and spirit. He started taking acting classes, worked his way through commercials and television series, and today is a successful actor in Hollywood films.

That same spirit that Brian found lives deep within all of us. What is your true passion? What would you do if you could do anything right now? Explore and discover your own natural swing.

By simply asking and answering those questions, you will awaken the deepest and most meaningful part of your existence. Changing your life in its entirety is not necessary. At the very least, begin to explore who you are and what you believe will make you happy. As a result, you will subconsciously make subtle, perhaps undetectable changes that will enrich your life.

You can experience passion and excitement through simple thoughts or dreams. It may be as simple as entertaining a crazy or adventurous idea, such as skydiving or bungee jumping. Perhaps you've imagined yourself pitching the seventh game of the World Series or winning a gold medal in the Olympics. Maybe you've been dreaming about taking that trip around the world. Your dreams represent the desires of your inner spirit.

Begin to trust yourself and find your own way of living. There is only one right way to do it—your way. Establish your own personal philosophy. Honor yourself and who you are by exploring and expressing your true nature. Your purpose for being is waiting to be discovered. You will know when you have found it.

•••

1. TRUST YOUR INSTINCTS. To find your natural swing, or true self, off the golf course, you must trust your instincts. This is a simple concept, yet it is difficult to put into practice. You must give yourself the freedom to be. Trusting your instincts involves listening to your inner voice. Listen for guidance and advice from the most reliable source available—you.

2. FIND YOUR OWN WAY. We often make decisions based on the influence of others and what they might think of us. These external energies will try to dictate how you live on the outside. However, they cannot dictate who you are inside. Challenge yourself to make decisions based on your feelings alone, independent of third parties, peers, and especially the negative voice in your mind. Focus on what you want. With regular practice, you will learn to trust yourself. Only then can you find your own way.

3. SEARCH YOUR SOUL. In your truest, most natural state, who are you? Where and when are you most yourself, with no fear of judgment or analysis from yourself or others? Think of situations in which you have felt complete comfort and ease. Why did you feel this way? For example, you may feel you are most yourself when you are alone at a secluded place where you can reflect. This may tell you that you are naturally an introspective person. Honor that and make space for it in your life.

PLAY ONE SHOT AT A TIME

"It is nothing new or original to say that golf is played one stroke at a time. But it took me many years to realize it."

Bobby Jones

"Staying in the present is the key to any golfer's game: once you start thinking about a shot you just messed up or what you have to do on the next nine to catch somebody, you're lost."

Paul Azinger

HOW often do you go to the golf course saying to yourself, "Today, I'm going to break eighty or ninety," or "I should beat this guy because I'm a better player." Or, as you walk to the first tee, you think you must hit a great tee shot to set the tone for a good round. At that one moment, your whole round is riding on that first shot. That's a lot of pressure.

Only one golf swing can take place at one moment in time. People claim they know how to multitask. To me, that translates into trying to do too many things at once, often sacrificing the quality of each individual activity.

Why does it seem that players who have never won a professional tour event often build up large leads, but eventually falter in the final round? It's probably because they get ahead of themselves, losing their focus and concentration.

An example of some thoughts that may enter such a player's mind: "I'm in the lead. This would be huge. I could use the money, Exemption status! All my years of practice, living out of a suitcase, and struggling on the mini-tour will finally pay off. I can finally prove I belong. Hang in there for only nine more holes. I'm finally going to make it."

The next thing you know, the golfer may hit a wayward shot or make a bogey. More thoughts creep in: "I lost a stroke. I've got to make that up. It might not be enough. It looks like people are starting to make a move. I can't lose this thing. I can't blow this."

At about this time, the anxiety and pressure have built up to an enormous level. The golfer has lost focus on the most important thing—hitting golf shots. The distractions and thoughts are overwhelming.

This sort of experience happens to all golfers, of all abilities. How many times have you blown the back nine after shooting a career best front nine, or shot a triple bogey after a birdie? Often, golfers begin to think about their final score. Or they find themselves dwelling on a poor shot made three holes prior, which then causes them to hit another poor shot.

Frank was a player who had a difficult time keeping his game together. Oftentimes the night before a round of golf, he couldn't sleep because he was so nervous. He sometimes walked up to the first tee worried about his final score, hoping that it wouldn't be embarrassing. If he hit a poor shot, he would mumble to himself, trying to figure out what he was doing wrong. As he stepped up to the next shot, he was often still thinking about the last one.

He also got distracted by the slightest of noises. If someone moved ever so slightly during his shot, he noticed and got very upset. That would linger for a few holes, affecting his play throughout.

The irony was that he carried his cell phone with him, which often rang, interrupting the play of others. He would always answer a call, and at times would conduct business on the golf course. By the time he finished a call and returned to his shot, he was still thinking about work, which adversely affected his play.

There is only one way to play golf: *one shot at a time.* All your energy must be focused on one moment. Eliminate distractions, let go of past shots, and center yourself. This will allow you to play your best golf.

At the end of the 2001 Masters, Tiger Woods took off his hat and covered his face while standing on the 18th green. During the interviews afterward, he was asked what he was feeling during that moment. Tiger responded, "I was attuned to each and every shot that I focused so hard on just that one shot. I finally realized I had no more to play. That's it. I'm done. I just won the Masters." He later said, "When you focus so hard on each and every shot, you kind of forget everything else." That's focus, and playing golf in the moment.

Even the best players in the world do not hit every shot perfectly. They will hit an errant shot out of bounds or into the water every now and then. The key is how they respond on the next shot. Golfers with the strongest mental games are able to let the prior shots go and start fresh on the next one. This is playing in the moment, or being present.

For the amateur golfer, the lesson is priceless. Treat each shot as if it's the only one you're taking and you will sense a deeper passion and commitment to that shot. You cannot change the past, so don't dwell on prior shots, whether good or bad. Nor can you affect the future, so don't think about the end score or a difficult hole coming up. All you can do is channel your energy to the present. Focus completely on the shot at hand.

I coached a former professional athlete who had a great enthusiasm for golf. She loved playing and desperately wanted to get better. She got frustrated by the occasional hole where she would shoot a high number, thinking it ruined her overall score.

We worked on isolating each shot as a unique, individual, stand-alone experience. *Each shot* was a new beginning, just like starting a new round. By playing in the moment, she was able to put her best effort forward on each and every shot. She learned to follow a poor shot or hole with a fresh outlook. As a result, she rarely had a series of poor shots or holes and was able to recover more consistently.

I challenge you to enjoy the *process* of golf. Appreciate a shot from a present-moment focus. The process of playing golf is the goal: the pre-shot ritual, grounding your body, developing a feel for the club, visualizing the shot you desire, and trusting yourself to create that shot. When you detach from the outcome (i.e., whether the ball goes in the hole or not), you will begin to capture the essence of the game. The spirit of golf exists in the way you play the game.

When you feel that you have been fully present and given your full attention and intention to the shot at hand, you have practiced the deepest, most rewarding part of golf.

Many times you hear how golfers play well but don't score well. Even at the professional level, you often hear in interviews after each round, "I'm hitting good shots, my putts are rolling well. They just aren't falling into the cup." These are the golfers who will achieve success in the long run, because they are focusing on the present moment.

They aren't dwelling on the past or worrying about the future. They know they are doing all the right things. With patience and continued practice of present-moment golf, the results and outcome will eventually take care of themselves.

It you play each shot one by one, with full presence and detachment from the outcome, your shots and scores will improve with an effortless ease. Once you strike the ball, let go. Let go of your attachment to the result. Let go of your judgment. Judgment will only diminish your spirit and lessen your experience.

Instead of judging your shot, be present and describe the shot. By not judging, I mean there's no such thing as a good, bad, or ugly shot. It's simply a shot. Observe the path of the ball and describe its movement. "The ball is going up in the air, reaching its apex, falling down to the ground, bouncing several times, and rolling to a stop." This will help you focus on one shot at a time and appreciate the process.

Even if the shot goes astray from your intended path, do not dwell on this as a negative occurrence. Instead, see it as an opportu-

nity. If you hit into a trap, view this as an opportunity to hit a great bunker shot. You are constantly creating more opportunities and chances to hit the next shot with total focus and concentration.

Imagine if you could enjoy and appreciate each and every moment you are on the golf course. It would always be fulfilling and joyful. Tap into all your senses. Focus on the moment. You will enjoy golf for what it is and not what it does.

Sometimes players are so engrossed in themselves and their performance that they don't even realize how beautiful it is on a golf course or how wonderful it is to spend time with family and friends. Notice nature and your surroundings. Breathe. Experience golf fully. The way I see it, if you are swinging a golf club or playing golf, compared to what is happening in some parts of the world, your life is OK. Enjoy the moment.

So imagine yourself standing on the tee of one of the world's most beautiful par-3s. [18] As the sun is setting, all you hear are the birds and nature. With all the time in the world, tee your ball up and take a deep breath. Start your ritual, visualize the shot you want, address the ball, and just let it go.

No matter what the outcome, savor the experience. If it goes into a trap, that's all right. If it goes in the water, that's OK too. If it goes in the hole, that'll be fine. It really doesn't matter because you're playing golf.

If we can all begin to approach the game like this, we will capture the essence of golf and have a deeper connection—with ourselves and with the world around us. If you are able to accomplish this simple exercise of being present, you will begin to experience golf like you never have before. You will begin to enjoy the game—*one shot at a time.* By letting go of the past and not worrying about the future, you will fully focus on the present—the most freeing experience of all.

EXERCISES

1. Clear your mind. If it is difficult for you to quiet your mind (e.g., letting go of prior shots, worrying about your score, concern about playing slowly or people watching), take three or four four-part breaths on the golf course. As you exhale, let all of your thoughts release and drift away.

2. Treat your shot as if it is the only shot you are going to take. Imagine that you will be able to play only one shot today.

3. Start your ritual with your trigger and a deep breath. As you exhale slowly and evenly, sense your body settling into your center.

4. Continue with your ritual and allow yourself to swing freely without thought or distraction.

5. Practice nonjudgment and complete detachment from outcome. Instead of judging it as a "good shot" or "bad shot," simply observe the ball in motion as it takes flight, lands, and rolls to a stop. Savor the experience of playing golf regardless of the outcome.

6. Take another deep breath. As you release your breath, release the shot. Enjoy the essence of golf. Be present with your shot.

PLAY ONE SHOT AT A TIME OFF THE GOLF COURSE

Turn off the autopilot
Be present now
Surrender to the moment

Peace, happiness, and tranquility can be experienced at any time, at any moment. They are things that can be tapped into regardless of your environment.

I moved from the San Francisco Bay Area to the Big Island of Hawaii several years ago. My goal was to find an environment conducive to a simple, happy lifestyle. I could surely achieve my goal of creating a satisfying and gratifying life for myself and my family if I lived in paradise!

What I noticed is that even though I now lived in one of the most beautiful places in the world, I still got caught up in the same daily stresses I felt when I lived in a busy metropolis. I noticed this poignantly when I once took my children to Kauna'oa (Mauna Kea) Beach, ranked the number-one beach in the world. As I held my infant son in my arms, blocking him from the sun's harm, and yelled at my five-year-old daughter to stop splashing, I looked out into the distance and noticed how the sky, ocean, and sand blended together in a continuum. At that moment, I saw every shade of blue.

It dawned on me: I wasn't living in the present. My mind was overloaded with so many thoughts—controlling my children, responsibilities at work, things to do at home, bills to pay, and deadlines everywhere—that I hadn't even noticed how blessed I was . . . to be with my children at one of the most tranquil, breathtakingly beautiful places in the world. I stopped. I took a deep breath, looked at my family, and smiled. I felt happiness in that moment.

What does it mean to live your life moment to moment? For some, it is simply being aware and conscious of each and every one of their experiences as they occur. Take a deep breath right now. Take a look around at where you are this moment—how are you holding this book, what are you wearing, how are you sitting or lying down? Notice your immediate surroundings and how you feel. You are bringing your consciousness to the moment and freeing your mind of the past and future. You may feel a sense of peace and tranquillity. Being aware of the present is the most powerful path to happiness.

You may have felt pure consciousness at various times in your life without even knowing it. Perhaps it was the first time you witnessed nature on a grand scale—the Grand Canyon, Yosemite's Half Dome, or Mount Everest. No words can describe your feelings. You are beyond awe.

At that moment, when you are breathless, you are living in the moment. All your thoughts dissolve, all your worries disappear, and you simply notice what is happening at that moment. This awakening is a powerful occurrence, and not only for that particular moment. It has an impact on your entire life. You know that you are alive.

You can experience these feelings every day simply by being present. Treat each moment as a miracle—as if you are always in the presence of grandeur, because in truth you are. Observe your world, take notice of who you are, slow down, and absorb. This exact moment is perfect as it is. Focus on the present and the rewards of your existence will overflow.

•••

1. *TURN OFF THE AUTOPILOT.* Living your life without true consciousness is like cruising on autopilot. It seems as if you are living, but you are actually just drifting from one place to another. Observe yourself when you seem overwhelmed or busy running errands. Are you trying to do everything at the same time? Challenge yourself to be conscious of what you are doing, thinking, and feeling, even during the most chaotic of times. You may find your life is not as complicated as you thought and that you actually have all the time in the world.

2. *BE PRESENT NOW.* No matter what you are doing (or not doing), notice this moment. As you read this sentence, recognize how this experience is unfolding for you—where you are, what you are doing, and how you are feeling. Regardless of what you are doing (even the most mundane of things such as vacuuming the house), put your full attention to it.

3. *SURRENDER TO THE MOMENT.* Focus on one thing at a time. Even when you have a list of to-do's, focus on doing one activity at a time. Tell yourself, "I am here now doing this one thing." Do not worry about the past or the future. Just focus on that one moment. You will then experience your life fully with total awareness, never missing a moment.

TRANSFORM YOUR GOLF GAME, TRANSFORM YOUR LIFE

"Sooner or later golfers who stick with the game long enough will almost always come to see it as a metaphor for life. But the word metaphor fails to do justice to all that golf has to teach us. I would go even further and say that, in its own way, golf is life and, not only that, "life condensed." If we choose to use it as such, I believe that golf, next to marriage and parenthood, can routinely be the greatest of life's learning opportunities."

M. Scott Peck

INNER PEACE ... Tiger Woods spoke of it when he won the 2000 U.S. Open at Pebble Beach, California. Calm ... David Duval felt it throughout the week he won the 2001 British Open. Both golfers experienced a sense of tranquillity, serenity, and ease during their victories.

As demonstrated by Tiger and David, all golfers can experience these feelings on the golf course by shifting their outlook and philosophy. Change your view of the world and begin to transform your golf game and your life.

Golf, by its nature, is a journey. In the beginning, you stand on the first tee with a stick and a ball. You hit the ball with the stick . . . walk to the ball and hit it again ... This continues some seventy, eighty, ninety, a hundred times before you return to the place where it all started.

In the physical world, you have not progressed at all. On an experiential level, you have journeyed far and beyond, through an infinite number of challenges, emotions, and experiences. The beauty of golf is the uniqueness of every shot, every hole, and every eighteen-hole experience. No two are ever the same.

We often forget that a journey is made up of singular moments. One cannot experience a full journey all at one time. Likewise, you cannot play eighteen holes of golf or live your entire life all at once.

True beauty is in the moment. This exact moment is the most important part of your journey.

How you play the game of golf is how you live your life. Most golfers look to external forces, such as the latest golf club or gadget, for answers to their hopes and desires for a better score.

Look inside, within your deeper self, and ask, "What is it that makes you feel passion, excitement, and fulfillment?"

Jackson played the game of golf with true passion. He loved every part of the game. However, his life off the golf course was quite the opposite. With a failing marriage and distant relationship to his children, Jackson experienced little joy off the links. He disliked his job and only did it to pay his bills and green fees.

I asked him to imagine living his life, all parts of his life, with the same passion and thrill that he felt hitting a perfect drive down the middle of the fairway. He began to see how his experience in golf would be great in his life off the golf course.

It's not only possible, it's natural. We all want to live joyful, fulfilling lives. If you have experienced joy or passion in golf, then it is possible to feel that same joy and passion off the golf course.

For most golfers, the perfect shot or a personal best round taps into those feelings. It is likely that you've experienced those feelings firsthand on the golf course. It is why we play the game. Seek those feelings in every part of your life—your career, family life, relationships, and personal growth.

On a deeper level, experience those feelings of elation even in the midst of golf shots that go astray, stressful times, and heated moments both on and off the golf course. There is always a place of calm and peace within a storm. Achieving success on the golf course is not necessarily scoring well or winning tournaments. Success is knowing that all those things *can* occur effortlessly as by-products of or afterthoughts to a deeper experience.

Golfers often try to emulate others. Don't try to be someone else. Be you. Explore who you are and be that person on the golf course. Inner peace is achieved when you know yourself and live your life accordingly.

Uncertainty is difficult to endure. People find it easier to keep a job they hate or remain in a destructive relationship than to seek a potentially better, though uncertain, situation. However, once you discover your true feelings, you can no longer fool your heart. You will change.

As I mentioned in the introduction, golf has been a transformational tool for me and for many others. After graduate school, I embarked on a career in management consulting. I felt this was the "right" job for me. I quickly found myself getting on an airplane every week, flying from San Francisco to New York on Monday, working sixteen-hour days, and then flying back from New York to San Francisco for the weekend.

I was in a constant state of exhaustion. I spent weekends trying to regain some semblance of a normal life. My relationship with my girlfriend suffered. We only had the weekends to spend together, and for much of that time I was working or trying to catch up on bills and paperwork. We often spent our time together fighting, even on the way to and from the airport. My relationships with friends became nonexistent. I had little energy to attend any social gathering.

Simultaneously, my golf game was paralleling my life. I had reached the point where my golf game had not only leveled off, but started to deteriorate. My scores soared and the game was no longer fun. I became very tense standing over the golf ball and had lost all confidence in my golf swing. I became so frustrated, I quit the game.

This drastic action was exactly what was needed. By taking time off from the game, I began to appreciate golf for what it generously offered to me. I realized that golf gave me more than I had ever thought: joy, peace, relaxation, exhilaration, challenge, creativity.

When I returned to golf four months later, I began to focus on the inner game—the mental aspects of golfing. As I experimented with relaxation techniques and ways to increase my focus and concentration, I felt a sense of freedom in my swing.

My golf game steadily improved. I realized that my best shots manifested when I trusted, listened to my intuition, and just "let go." The process that led me to that critical moment is now called the Seven Principles of Golf.

The principles that helped me improve my golf game began to affect my life. Once I got my golf game going, my life started to follow. I took time off from work to reflect and explore my potential. I focused on the inner game of life.

I achieved balance by sleeping and eating well and getting in shape physically. I practiced yoga and meditation and took a personal retreat. My relationship with my girlfriend took an exponential leap as we moved in together and got engaged five months after that.

As I explored and discovered new ways to connect, I started listening to my intuition and trusting the process. My inner voice kept telling me to follow my passion for golf and helping others achieve their potential. When I finally "let go" and trusted my inner self, I began to share the Seven Principles of Golf in golf clinics, through motivational speaking, and through books and instructional DVDs.

I transformed my golf game and simultaneously transformed my life. The Principles certainly apply to your golf game, but perhaps more importantly they will have an impact on your life off the golf course:

Balance. Seek balance in your life. Balance your work, your family, and all the things you love to do, including golf. Balance it all for a more fulfilling experience of life.

Feel. Listen to your intuition or inner voice—it's usually right. Your inner voice reflects your deeper feelings and true self.

Visualization. Knowing what you want is the key to visualization. Ask yourself "What do I want?" continually in reference to all parts of your life—financial, emotional, physical, spiritual. Picture what you want in your mind's eye and then release it or let go. Don't get in the way or sabotage yourself.

Ritual. Establish and practice a daily ritual that helps you connect with yourself. In as little as five minutes, a ritual will have a tremendous impact on your life. Rituals with others such as spouses, family, and friends will help you connect with them.

Natural Swing. Find your own way. Discover and explore your true passion. Experiment and imagine yourself doing whatever you want in the world. What would that look like? Natural swing is about knowing who you are and honoring it every moment.

One Shot at a Time. Be present. Let go of the past; don't worry about the future. Focus on the moment.

Transform Your Golf Game, Transform Your Life. Take one ounce of the passion you have for this simple game called golf and begin to spread it to other parts of your life. Those other parts will naturally begin to flourish and blossom. Likewise, once you create the life you want, golf and everything else will go along for the ride.

Transformation occurs as a by-product of other things changing. One cannot decide to transform and then do it. It happens as you shift other aspects of your life. In golf, transformation occurs when your perspective changes from an attachment focus to one of present-moment experience. Once you focus on the process and experience of golf, you will then achieve a higher level of performance.

Transformation in your golf game is the same as transformation in your life. As one occurs, so does the other. Transforming your life is the experience of shifting your perspective to be your true self. Once you focus on who you are and what you want, you will then achieve your true desires. Connect with your inner self and let go. You will then begin to experience consciousness, both on and off the golf course.

EXERCISES

1. Answer these questions: What do you enjoy most about golf (e.g., elation, excitement, thrill, challenge)? What do you love in life (e.g., sports, traveling, hobbies, parenting)? Combine your answers into a general feeling or sensation and center it in your body.

2. Visualize yourself experiencing those feelings during every shot you take.

3. Heighten your senses. See the lush, green, rolling fairways, artistically dotted with white sand bunkers. Listen for the birds. Feel the wind flowing around you. Smell the grass and the air. Taste the perfect shot.

4. Treat each shortcoming as the creation of an opportunity. If you hit your ball into a greenside sand trap, see it as a chance to use your sand wedge to hit a great bunker shot. If you hit your next shot into the fringe, see it as an opportunity to be creative and hit a great chip shot.

5. View the golf experience as a reflection of your life experience and vice versa. Transform the way you play golf and you'll transform the way you live your life.

6. Reach your potential, both on and off the golf course.

TRANSFORM YOUR GOLF GAME, TRANSFORM YOUR LIFE OFF THE GOLF COURSE

Trust the process
Embrace the journey
Transform your life

Golf and life are synonymous.

When Steve attended our golf program, he was at a crossroads in his life. He had just turned forty-two, was still single, and had just quit his job as an accountant, a job he had grown to despise. He was feeling unsure about his future. There was uncertainty in virtually all parts of his life—career, relationships, and home. It also manifested in his golf game.

Steve was a scratch golfer and had experienced success at the amateur level in his home state. As he hit golf balls on the range, he began to shank the ball. He was baffled. He said he had never done that before. His dad, who was also participating in the program and standing next to him, confirmed that he had never seen him do that either. Steve set up for the next shot—another shank. And another and another. With each successive shot, he tried harder and grew increasingly frustrated and upset. He lost total confidence in his swing and had no idea what he was doing.

I pulled him aside and offered him some guidance. I told him that he was at a challenging stage in his life and that the uncertainty in his life was also showing up in his golf game. Tension and stress had trickled from his life and career to his golf swing. The more he tried to force things with life, the more difficult it became. It was the same with his golf swing.

He knew that he was thinking too much and trying too hard. I challenged him to pause, explore his passions in life, and discover what he really wanted to do. After our conversation, he returned to hitting golf balls. In the process, he forgot about his golf swing and simply let it go . . . straight down the middle.

Everyone has a higher purpose in life. You have a special power within you that makes you a unique, passionate individual, and it is up to you to discover that person. How do you do this? You have already begun. You've chosen to read this book and explore your growth on and off the golf course. The reasons you play golf most likely reflect the level of stimulation you seek in your life.

As you gain a deeper understanding of this, learn to embrace everything in your life—good or bad, happy or sad, exciting or mundane. Accept yourself and your life as it is, without judgment. You will realize your life's journey is unfolding perfectly. All your experiences, feelings, and emotions are exactly as they are meant to be—always.

Accept any misfortune or shortcoming as the universe's way of creating new opportunities specifically for you. Great growth and learning occur in difficult times, more so than under any other circumstance. You will gain a deeper understanding of what is truly important in your life. When faced with adversity, I am reminded of what is most important to me—being myself all the time. Accept your existence as a whole and you will begin to transform your life effortlessly. Your true self will surface naturally and you will realize you are already full and complete.

•••

1. TRUST THE PROCESS. The universe is weaving a one-of-a-kind experience for you. It is evolving with purpose and intent. Take a deep breath and observe the beauty of nature, which will remind you of your relationship to magnificence and creation. The process by which everything grows and exists is purposeful. Know in your heart that this process will support you.

2. EMBRACE THE JOURNEY. Accept every moment of every day as it is supposed to be. Turn blame into acceptance—of yourself, others, and circumstances in your life. When you experience a tough time or a shortcoming, view it as an opportunity to learn and grow. If you lose your job, look at it as an opportunity to do something new or what you've always wanted to do but were afraid to do. Remind yourself that you are on a hero's journey, and no matter what happens, it is always purposeful.

3. TRANSFORM YOUR LIFE. Shift your outlook and philosophy from one of the impossible to one of the possible. Your life will change as soon as you believe it can. Transform your life by simply expecting passion in all aspects of it. Apply some or all of the Seven Principles of Golf to all parts of your life. Inspire yourself to achieve your potential and the highest level of fulfillment and growth in every part of your life.

SOME CLOSING THOUGHTS

"Never hurry, never worry, and always remember to smell the flowers along the way."

Walter Hagen

GOLF has a magnetic, almost spiritual quality to it. Those who have experienced golf know exactly what this means. For every eighty to one hundred "terrible" strokes in a round of golf, there may be only one great shot. If you played any other sport and experienced that ratio of success to failure, you would quit. However, in golf, the number of great shots is irrelevant. It only takes one great shot to entice a golfer back for more.

Not everyone can slam-dunk a basketball like Michael Jordan or throw a football like John Elway or kick a soccer ball like Mia Hamm. However, in the game of golf, *anyone* can hit a shot as pure as Tiger Woods or Annika Sorenstam, regardless of ability or skill. Even pure beginners can experience hitting a perfect shot every now and then.

The shot, in and of itself, is unimportant. What brings a golfer back time and again is the anticipation and hope that the next shot can be "perfect." *Perfect* describes a shot that is effortless, almost surreal. The swing is easy, your mind is clear, and your heart beats uncontrollably as the ball takes flight, like a rocket exploding off the club. There is no other feeling like it.

I see this in my golf academy all the time, when students clear their minds, let go, and experience a perfect shot. "Wow!" or "Yes!" or "That was it!" or "Pure" is what we hear often. The elation experienced during a perfect shot gets into your heart and soul. You memorize that feeling and imprint it into your mind, body, and spirit. It is so strong that even in the worst of times you remember that feeling and long for it to return, perhaps on the next shot or the one after. Though the next "perfect" shot may not manifest for a round or two, the anticipation or simply the thought of it happening again drives golfers to a state bordering on obsession.

The Seven Principles of Golf are not really about golf. They are about individual potential and power. If one can achieve a perfect shot in golf, then one can achieve a perfect shot in life. Discovering and exploring one's potential is the key. Once this process begins, then one's true self emerges. This is truly the perfect shot.

ACKNOWLEDGMENTS

I would like to thank all those who have provided me with guidance and support along the journey of conceiving, writing, and publishing this book:

Jennifer Levesque, my editor, who did a fantastic job nurturing the book along, all while being pregnant herself during the process. Keith Witmer, whose wonderful illustrations have added so much to the spirit of the book. Pamela Geismar, for your creativity and style in design. My agent, Rita Rosenkranz, for your advice and energy in putting together the perfect package. Michael Jacobs, Abrams President & CEO; Leslie Stoker, Publisher of Stewart, Tabori & Chang; Steve Tager, Senior Vice President; and the rest of the Abrams/Stewart, Tabori & Chang group who believed in The Seven Principles of Golf and have made the entire process fun and exciting from start to finish.

Friends Mary Tiegreen and Hubert Pedroli for your limitless energy, encouragement, and good thoughts from the very beginning. Mary Embry, who first helped me explore the possibilities. Our resort and golf course hosts on the Big Island of Hawaii for their partnership in sharing the Spirit of Golf with golfers from around the world. My team at the Spirit of Golf Academy, who with boundless energy continue to share my vision with others.

My parents, who have supported me and my desire to create and pioneer a new concept in lieu of the traditional path. My children, Maya and Eric, who inspire me every day to be better as an individual and father. And my loving wife, partner, and best friend, Darien: I am so glad that we are making this journey together.

As a special thank you for buying this book, we would like to offer you our exclusive bonus report, "Darrin Gee's Top 10 Secrets to a Great Golf Game," absolutely free. Visit www.darringee.com to register for your complimentary copy.

Now that you've read the book, take your game to the next level with Darrin Gee's two-volume DVD set, *Mastering the Mental Game of Golf.* Darrin demonstrates the Seven Principles and teaches you how to apply them to your putting stroke and full swing. Also included are two bonus 16-page companion guides with step-by-step exercises.

An engaging and entertaining speaker, Darrin is available to motivate and inspire your group to reach their potential and achieve peak performance in all aspects of life, including professional careers and personal growth. To book Darrin for your event, call (808) 887-6800.

To experience the Seven Principles of Golf first-hand, visit Darrin Gee's Spirit of Golf Academy, the premier golf school in the country focusing on the mental game, located at top resorts and golf courses on the Big Island of Hawaii.

To order the DVD or for more information, please contact us at:

Darrin Gee's Spirit of Golf Academy
P.O. Box 6886
Kohala Coast, Island of Hawaii 96743

Website: www.darringee.com
Email: info@darringee.com

Reservations (808) 887-6800
Toll-free (866) GOLF-433
Facsimile (808) 887-2893

ABOUT THE AUTHOR

Darrin Gee developed the Seven Principles of Golf after becoming frustrated with his own game. As he focused on improving his mental and inner game skills, he was amazed by the dramatic shift in his performance and its effect on other areas of his life.

In 2000, he moved to the Big Island of Hawaii and launched Darrin Gee's Spirit of Golf Academy. He has received national recognition as a leading authority on mental and inner golf mastery, and has been credited for bringing more people to the game.

A sought-after motivational speaker at corporate events and various organizations, Darrin's background includes marketing, sales, management consulting, and corporate strategy for major corporations. He has been a consultant and advisor to companies at all stages of development.

Darrin received his MBA from Northwestern University and holds a BA in psychology from UCLA. Darrin lives on the Big Island of Hawaii with his wife and business partner, Darien Hsu Gee, and their two children, Maya and Eric.